Children in the Early Church

Children in the Ancient World, the New Testament and the Early Church

Children in the Early Church

Children in the Ancient World, the New Testament and the Early Church

W.A.Strange

paternoster
press

Typeset by WestKey Ltd., Falmouth, Cornwall
Printed in Great Britain by Clays Ltd., Bungay, Suffolk

Contents

Preface

The idea for this book began with a question: if Jesus had so much to say about children, why did the early church have so little to say about them? How was it that the church came to be so silent on the subject of children that we cannot tell, for instance, whether or not the first Christians baptized infants?

That initial question soon generated others. Was it in fact the case that Jesus had much to say about children? Was the early church indeed so completely silent about them? And what did children and childhood mean in the culture of the New Testament world? The chapters which follow attempt to frame an answer to those questions.

It is necessary to cast the net fairly wide in framing this answer, and we need to take a reasonably detailed look at the culture of the time in order not to misunderstand what either Jesus or the first Christians said about children. Social scientists have argued that 'childhood' is a social construct, not an unchanging given of nature, but a way of interpreting human experience and development. Philippe Ariès, in his seminal book *Centuries of Childhood* (1960, ET 1973), pioneered the study of childhood as a historical theme, and proposed the thesis that the recognition of childhood as a separate stage of life was a discovery of post-Renaissance society. His thesis has been modified and criticized by subsequent writers, but he alerted all who would look at the subject to the possibility that previous ages may have had quite different presuppositions about childhood from our own. We cannot simply read the texts which concern us without trying to uncover those presuppositions; otherwise we may seriously misunderstand what they are saying.

In several respects this book had to be restricted as it was written, or it would have grown beyond the bounds set for it in the initial questions with which its author began.

One area in which its scope had to be restricted was that of the biblical material. In examining the gospels, some readers may think that I take an over-confident view of the authenticity of what is said in them about the words and deeds of Jesus, and that this book therefore makes too many assumptions about how well we can know the Jesus of history through the gospel record. However, to enter caveats and long justifications at every point would not only have made this book much lengthier but would also have turned it into a different sort of book altogether. In chapter two I assumed that there has been some interpretation by the evangelists and their communities of Jesus' words and deeds, although it will be clear also that I accept the basic material of sayings and actions as authentic. A reader who would wish to give the evangelists or their communities a more far-reaching role in creating this material will need to make the necessary adjustments as they read this chapter.

To keep the book within bounds it was also necessary to cut the story short at some point. We need, certainly, to look beyond the confines of the New Testament and into the life of the early church. A reader whose prime interest is in the New Testament should bear with this for two reasons. One is that some trends, already observable in the New Testament, can be seen more clearly when their outcome is made evident in the post-New Testament Christian community; as discussions of infant baptism have always shown, when the New Testament material is ambiguous, later practice and belief may shed light on that original Christian generation. The other consideration is that the life of the early church has an interest of its own; we are able to observe the first Christians struggling with the problems and opportunities of being Christ's people in a pagan society. But in this book we cannot follow the story of children in the church all the way to the present day. Readers wanting to investigate the development of the child's place in the church through the centuries will find much that is helpful in *The Church and Childhood* by D. Wood (ed).

I have had no conscious thesis to argue in this book, though my own convictions and conclusions will no doubt be obvious to the reader. The purpose of the book is to make the relevant material available and comprehensible, and I hope that it will be of use to those who are concerned with Christian ministry among children today.

I would like to thank the Board of Mission of the Church in Wales for permission to use, in altered form, material which I contributed to a report on the admission of children to Communion; and the Church in Wales' Board of Ministry for a grant which enabled me to continue work on the book. Some material in chapter three has appeared, in a different form, in *The Journal of Beliefs and Values*.

To this I would add my thanks to Dr David Gill for his helpful comments on a draft of chapter one.

Without my wife's patience this book could not have been written, and without her careful reading of the various drafts it would have been greatly lacking in coherence and intelligibility. And finally, I have to thank Oliver and Harry, who have taught me more about children, and reminded me of more about childhood, than any number of books.

References

It has been my aim to keep the text clear of footnotes, and to avoid long discussions or debates with those who have already written on this subject. But it is important for readers to be able to follow up points in an argument and to check for themselves the assertions which I have made. I have, therefore, included references to biblical passages, ancient Greek and Latin authors, Jewish sources, early Christian writers, and modern authors.

Biblical passages are referred to in the conventional way. Most of the Greek and Latin writings used in this book can be found easily in the Loeb Classical Library series (editions of the texts with English translations on facing pages). Where there is no Loeb edition, but where there is another English translation, the text will indicate that. The works of the two Jewish writers, Philo and Josephus, are also available in Loeb editions. There are various English translations of the early Christian writers. These can be found in *The Oxford Dictionary of the Christian Church* by F.L. Cross (ed.).

References to modern authors use the author-date system. Instead of a reference to the title of a work, the reference is given simply as a name (the author), a date (of publication) and a number (the page number). The full details of the work can then be found in the Bibliography.

NE: Some of the most significant Christian texts to which reference is made in chapters three and four can be found in a readily-accessible form in *A New Eusebius, documents illustrating the history of the church to AD 337* by J. Stevenson and W.H.C. Frend (ed.), (2nd edn. 1987). Where a text is to be found in *A New Eusebius*, the reference is given as *NE*(page number).

Chapter 1

Children in the World of the New Testament

The first Christians lived in a world very different from our own, and when we read what the New Testament writers have to say about children, we need to know something at least of what it meant to be a child in the first century in Judaea, or Ephesus, or Rome. From the adult's point of view, what did people at the time think about their children? Or, from the child's perspective, what was it like to be a child in a household of the first century?

These questions are important, but are difficult to answer, mainly because people in the first century were not as reflective as we are about the nature of childhood and its importance in human development. In consequence, there are few books from the ancient world dealing specifically with children, and those we have are mainly concerned with education, its aims and problems. The first surviving work devoted to analysing education and improving the upbringing of children is Quintilian's *Education of an Orator (Institutio Oratoriae)*, written in the late first century. The first Christian work to offer systematic advice on child-rearing was written by John Chrysostom (c.347-407), in his little book entitled: *On the Vainglory of the World and on the Education of Children* (ET Laistner 1951).

What we can discover about children has therefore to be taken very largely from incidental comments made by authors writing on other topics, authors who drop hints or asides about children into their writings. Some are factual; others fictional. But all have value in showing us the attitudes of the ancients towards children and their assumptions about children. The lack of much direct writing about the children of the ancient world is not all our loss; it means that what we read is often a description of things as they were, rather than a telling of someone's theories about child-rearing. If the only text about children to survive from our culture was, say, that of Dr Spock, future historians might get a very misleading picture of how children were brought up in our times, not only because ideas change and advice on child-rearing becomes as dated as any other, but also because at any one point not everyone would agree with the view of a particular authority.

When we get down to reading what people from the ancient world have left us as a guide to their understanding of children, we find it puzzling. There is an appealing tenderness in much writing, for example in epitaphs which give us a moving glimpse of the feelings of parents towards the children they had lost through death. But alongside this, there was also a casual and almost off-hand brutality in the day-to-day treatment of the young. Newborn babies were often exposed to die on city rubbish heaps, and even the children of caring parents were beaten regularly and severely. One of the aspects of the world of the New Testament which we shall have to try to understand is the existence, side by side, of an undoubted love for children with a general acceptance of the harsh and cruel treatment of children.

To understand the place of children in the New Testament and in the early church, we need to look at the evidence we have, not only from specifically Christian texts, the New Testament itself and the writings of the early Christians, but also from non-Christian sources, both Jewish and Gentile, because these will illuminate for us the culture in which the early Christians lived.

The writings which make up the New Testament span a wide variety of places and cultures. The experience of Jewish children, for instance, was different from that of Gentiles. Boys, generally in both Jewish and Gentile families, did not have the same course through childhood as their sisters, since boys and girls were being prepared for quite separate roles in society. A child growing up in a cosmopolitan city such as Rome would have a very different sort of childhood from a child in a small agricultural community. Family sizes and kinship structures varied widely from place to place. And inevitably, we are better informed about the lives of the wealthy, who have left their record in literature or on monuments, than we are about the poor, who in every age disappear with little trace. Whatever we say, therefore, about children and childhood in the time of the New Testament runs the risk of oversimplifying a complex picture. We also find ourselves concentrating on certain groups simply because we know more about them, whether or not they were typical of the wider population. We should perhaps speak of the worlds rather than the world of the New Testament, to remind us that there were different cultural, language, and religious groups to be found around the Mediterranean in the first century.

This chapter will look in turn at the Jewish and the Gentile worlds. In both these worlds there were distinctions between rich and poor, and urban and rural. The Christian movement began in a Jewish setting and moved to embrace Gentiles. So, to understand the place of children in the ministry of Jesus and the life of the early church, we should try to understand some of the differences between a Jewish and a Gentile childhood.

But first we shall look at the features of childhood which we might expect to be common to both Jewish and Gentile cultures, and in both urban and rural settings.

Common Features of Childhood in the Ancient World

If we could suddenly transport ourselves to the Mediterranean of the first century AD, we would probably be surprised at just how many small children there were. Families had to be large, because infant mortality was so high. It has been estimated that less than half of all children survived to their fifth birthday, and only forty per cent survived to the age of twenty. In consequence, a couple would need to produce five children in order to ensure the likelihood of two surviving to childbearing age (Wiedemann 1989 15f.).

The perinatal period was especially hazardous. It was only on the eighth day that Roman girls received their name; boys on the ninth, the *dies lustricus* – 'day of the purifying sacrifice' – so called because the children were ceremonially cleansed on that day by a sacrifice offered on their behalf. A Jewish boy was circumcised on the eighth day. It was as if the newborn infant was so uncertain of life that there was no point in admitting its existence until the first precarious week was over.

At some periods, indeed, there was much concern that the birth rate was dropping to such a low level that the population was failing to reproduce itself. This concern was particularly acute for the ruling elite of the Empire. The Roman state enacted legislation from the time of Julius Caesar onwards to encourage larger families, at least among Roman citizens. This concern reminds us that large numbers of children were necessary to maintain the population, and it suggests that steps were taken by some couples to limit family size. Couples had two possible ways of family limitation: infanticide and contraception.

Infanticide was practised, probably on a wide scale. It was implicitly condoned by most sections of society in the Roman Empire, and not prohibited by Roman law. Deformed children were regularly exposed, and girls were also frequently abandoned. A husband in Egypt, writing to his wife in the first century BC, gave advice which was stark but not unusual: 'If you chance to bear a child, and it is a boy, let it be; if it is a girl, expose it' (*Oxyrhynchus Papyrus* 744). The exposing of children is one of the aspects of the ancient world which we find most disturbing. But we must remember that some parents were driven to this desperate expedient by dire poverty. The standard of living of most people was at a level which we would today associate with the Third World. An extra mouth to feed was a serious problem for many families, and in parts of the Empire where a small family holding had to be divided equally between brothers, there was a strong incentive to ensure that not too many should survive.

Infanticide was not the only answer to the problem of too many mouths to feed. Contraception of various forms was available in the ancient world, though there is some controversy about how effective it was in practice. To judge from the medical authorities whose works have survived, couples used herbal preparations as forms of birth control to reduce fertility or induce abortions (Riddle 1991 3-32).

The Jews, in this as in many other matters, differed radically from their Gentile contemporaries. Jewish law and custom looked with abhorrence on these practices which seem to have been commonplace among Gentiles; on infanticide in particular. The law of Moses was taken to condemn abortion (Exod. 21:22-5), and this also effectively ruled out the use of numerous contraceptive preparations which were intended to abort the foetus. Some prophylactic contraceptive methods were known and used by Jews, and were approved if the purpose was to protect the woman's health, for instance to prevent a nursing mother conceiving (Safrai 1976 764). Infanticide and abortion were condemned by Jewish writers, notably the first century Jewish philosopher, Philo of Alexandria (*Special Laws* 3.110-119). Philo in fact distinguished early-term abortion from late-term abortion. He considered early-term abortion a form of injury, and claimed it explained why the Law prescribed merely a fine in Exodus 21:22-5. However, when the foetus was fully formed, abortion was a form of murder. And so, of course, was the exposure of infants. His words help us envisage what the exposure of children really meant:

> As to the charges of murder in general and murder of their own children in particular the clearest proofs of their truth are supplied by their parents. Some of them do the deed with their own hand; with monstrous barbarity and cruelty they stifle and throttle the first breath which the infants draw or throw them into a river or into the depths of the sea, after attaching

some heavy substance to make them sink more quickly under its weight. Others take them to be exposed in some desert place, hoping, they themselves say, that they may be saved, but leaving them actually to suffer the most distressing fate. (Philo, *Special Laws* 3.114f.)

Jews seem not to have taken steps to limit family size. Indeed, since propagating the race was a major responsibility, and later Jewish tradition would hold that failing to do so was as bad as shedding blood or despising God's image, we should suppose that their families were in general large ones.

The fact remains that, apart from occasional complaints about decline, the population of the Empire did sustain itself, which meant the birth of considerable numbers of children. And there were vital economic reasons for begetting a substantial progeny. For us, children are wanted because parents wish to share their love with a new generation. It has been aptly said that in our culture, children are a kind of pet. But in the ancient world, as in many cultures today, most people needed children so that there would be someone to look after them in their old age.

The wealthy classes had money to ensure their well-being in old age. They did not therefore need children in the same way as the peasantry. Perhaps this is why their families were smaller, and why successive emperors felt obliged to encourage them to have more children. The subsistence farmers who must have made up a large proportion of the Empire's population needed no outside encouragement to have the largest family that they could afford. Juvenal (late first century), writing in one of his poems of the ideal peasant family, envisaged a sturdy household of husband and wife (the wife in confinement), their four children playing around the home in the company of a fifth child born to one of the slaves (perhaps by the father of the house). Meanwhile, the older children would be working in the fields (Juvenal, *Satires* 14.166-172). Peasant families may not always have been quite so fecund, but that at least is what a Roman of the first century thought a farmer's family *ought* to be like. Children were expensive, and sometimes the poor must have been driven to expose their children for that reason. But they were a necessary investment, and the need to provide for the future must have ensured that sufficient children were born.

If we would be surprised at the large numbers of young children, we would be surprised, too, at the way they were taught and educated. In all societies, children have to be taught to acquire the skills and knowledge essential for them to survive as adults. But in the ancient world, this task of education was approached on a very different basis from ours. We shall look in more detail at the content of education when we examine Jewish and Gentile upbringing separately, but some basic assumptions about children and their education were shared across the two communities. Education was not seen as assisting the child in its growing awareness of its surroundings, and helping the child cope with concepts of increasing complexity and abstraction. Education of children was generally seen as more akin to training an animal.

If that judgment sounds too harsh, we should look at some of the things said about the rearing of children. The great philosopher Plato himself had compared bringing up a child to taming an animal:

> Of all wild creatures, the child is the most intractable; for insofar as it, above all others, possesses a fount of reason that is as yet uncurbed, it is a treacherous, sly and most insolent creature. Wherefore the child must be strapped up, as it were, with many bridles. (Plato, *Laws* 808D)

After reading Plato's rather jaundiced view of children, we might wonder whether we would have a fairer picture of the place of children in the ancient world if we had more material or indeed any relevant material written by women. How much did (male) theorists of education in the ancient world actually have to do with children on a day-to-day basis? Some, no doubt, had a solid basis of experience behind their observations, and we should put Quintilian, about whom we shall have more to say later, in this category. One of the greatest gaps in our knowledge concerns what women thought about children, especially since women had the major part in child-rearing in the youngest years. We wonder if they heeded the theorizing advocates of harsh discipline, resented them and rebelled, or, through sheer ignorance of the whole matter, treated their young children with great compassion because they had such a short period to enjoy them.

The assumption that raising a child was like taming or breaking-in an animal found expression in practical advice to parents. Advice on the practice of child-rearing regularly advocated a discipline which would seem extremely severe to us. We find this in the Jewish tradition in the book of Proverbs:

> A father who spares the rod hates his son, but one who loves his son brings him up strictly. Folly is deep-rooted in the hearts of children; a good beating will drive it out of them. Do not withhold discipline from a boy; take the stick to him, and save him from death. If you take the stick to him yourself, you will be preserving him from Sheol. (Prov. 13:24; 22:15; 23:13f.)

No doubt the exhortations of Proverbs were taken quite literally by many Jewish fathers (Safrai 1976 770f.). The practice advocated by Proverbs is referred to by the writer of the letter to the Hebrews. Drawing on the common experience of childhood shared by his readers, he could remind them of the 'painful' discipline which they had suffered at the hands of their fathers, for their own good (Heb.12:7-11). He could expect that they would all know what it meant to have been beaten by their father during childhood.

The beating of children as a form of discipline was also common in Gentile society. In the home, the father's authority was (in theory) unquestioned in most communities. At Rome, this authority was formalized as the *patria potestas*, the fatherly authority which extended to power of life and death over his children. By the first century AD, Roman fathers no longer had the legal right, which they had had in an earlier period, to put their children to death, although it was still legal to expose unwanted newborn infants. In the Greek culture which predominated in the eastern part of the Empire, fathers seem to have claimed a more limited authority, extending only until the age of eighteen (Kleijwegt 1991 58f.).

There were in all probability some indulgent parents, like those described by Pliny the Younger in the late first century (*Letters* 4.2) who allowed their children whatever luxuries and indulgences they could afford. But there were equally certainly parents, fathers in particular, who brought up their children under a disciplinary regime which we should consider brutal. At school, if children were sent there, they could expect little better. The schoolmaster considered corporal punishment, administered often and with severity, to be essential to his work (Quintilian, *Inst.Or.* 1.3.16f.).

When we read how parents treated their children, or how they were willing to let them be treated, we wonder whether they loved them. The answer must be that they did. But for them tenderness and harshness could exist side by side. There is plenty of evidence from literature and from funeral monuments that adults were attached to children, and genuinely cared for them. There is some indication that tenderness towards children may have increased in first-century Roman society. As an instance, there is this touching epitaph which the Roman poet Martial wrote on the death of his slave-child, Erotion, aged four or five:

> Let not the sod too stiffly stretch its girth
> Above those limbs, erstwhile so free;

> Press lightly on her form, dear mother Earth,
> Her little footsteps lightly fell on thee.
> (Martial, *Epigrams*, 5.34)

A clear example of parental affection is the letter of consolation which Plutarch (c.46-c.120 AD) wrote to his wife on the death of their two-year-old daughter ('Consolation to His Wife' *Moralia* Loeb edn. 7 575-605). It is stylized and formal, almost an essay on using philosophy to provide proper consolation. Yet through the formal conventions, real feeling and a transparently genuine grief are quite obvious in Plutarch's letter, as in this passage, in which Plutarch recalls their daughter's personality:

> I know what great satisfaction lay in this - that after four sons the longed-for daughter was born to you, and that she made it possible for me to call her by your name. Our affection for children so young has, furthermore, a poignancy all its own: the delight it gives is quite pure and free from all reproach. She had herself, moreover, a surprisingly natural gift of mildness and good temper, and her way of responding to friendship and of bestowing favours gave us pleasure while it afforded us an insight into her kindness. (Plutarch, 'Consolation' 2.)

But the most moving expression of parental love which has come down to us from antiquity is from a Christian source, and it is perhaps no coincidence that it occurs in one of the very few sources in which a woman speaks for herself. In or around 203 AD, two Christian women were martyred in the city of Carthage in North Africa, by being thrown to the beasts in the arena. One was a well-born young woman called Perpetua, and the other was her maid Felicitas. Perpetua had a young baby, and Felicitas gave birth while in prison. Perpetua wrote down her impressions of the prison, together with her dreams and visions as the end approached, and this work, as well as telling us much about martyrdom, tells us a great deal about the feelings of a mother for her child. Here we have none of the literary and philosophical conceits which we find in more polished writers, but we hear a very brave and rather frightened young woman speak in her own voice.

After her arrest, Perpetua found herself in prison:

> A few days later we were lodged in the prison; and I was terrified, as I had never before been in such a dark hole. What a difficult time it was! With the crowd the heat was stifling; then there was the extortion of the soldiers; and to crown all, I was tortured with worry for my baby there. (*Martyrdom of Saints Perpetua and Felicitas 3*, Musurillo 1972 109)

Later, the deacons Tertius and Pomponius bribed the soldiers to move the women to a better part of the prison:

> Everyone then left that dungeon and shifted for himself. I nursed my baby, who was faint with hunger. In my anxiety, I spoke to my mother about the child, I tried to comfort my brother, and I gave the child in their charge...Then I got permission for my baby to stay with me in prison. At once I recovered my health, relieved as I was of my worry and anxiety over the child. My prison had suddenly become a palace, so that I wanted to be there rather than anywhere else. (*Martyrdom 3*, Musurillo 1972 109f.)

The last Perpetua saw of her baby son was at the hearing of her case before the governor, when her father brought him to the court to try to persuade Perpetua to relent and offer the sacrifice to the Emperor which would save her life. When she was condemned and returned to prison, her father kept the baby, and a few days later Perpetua died in the arena.

Here is a different tone from that of the moralists and theorists whose works form the bulk of our information on children in the ancient world. If we needed evidence for genuine and deep affection of a parent for her child, it is here in these simple expressions of feeling which we owe to a woman about to die.

So, we can see that there was real love between parents and children. But there was brutality, too. Because, fond though people in the ancient world could be of children, they did not think them amenable to reason. Force seemed the only means of training children in the way they should go, and therefore the educative task was seen as being similar to training an animal.

Gentiles in the Greek world argued that because a child could not speak, it was lacking in reason: the Greek word '*logos*' having the double meaning of 'word' or 'speech' and 'reason'. This perception of the irrationality of children seems to explain the resort to force which was a universal feature of ancient society, Greek and Roman, Gentile and Jewish.

Children in the Jewish World

Jewish people in the ancient world did not all have the same attitudes and outlook. We might guess quite reasonably that Jews living in an urban Gentile setting such as the cities of the eastern Mediterranean, would have had rather different attitudes from those working the land in the small peasant communities of Galilee or Judaea. Our sources, some quite recently discovered, show us a diversity of outlooks even within Palestine itself. The discovery of the Dead Sea Scrolls, for instance, has revealed to us a set of Jewish people holding beliefs and practising a way of life quite different from the mainstream of Judaism as we know it from the later records of the rabbis. So we must beware of oversimplifying the picture of Judaism in the time of the New Testament. We must beware also of assuming that what was true of Jewish belief and practice several centuries later, when the traditions of the rabbis began to be written down and codified, was true in the first century.

Keeping in mind the dangers of oversimplifying a complex culture and of reading back later conditions into the New Testament period, some things can be said about children and their place in the life of the Jewish community in the first century.

Children as the Assurance of the Future

By the time of Christ's birth, the Jewish people were not all living in Palestine; and had not been for centuries. It was nearly six hundred years since Nebuchadnezzar had taken Jerusalem, broken down the walls and destroyed the temple. But although the kingdom of Judah was destroyed, the Jewish people survived as a recognizable entity; and not only in their own land. Communities of Jews were scattered all over the known world, and wherever they went they were able to retain their identity, sustaining their ancestral faith and their life as a nation.

One of the elements of their life which enabled them to survive and to prosper in this remarkable way, was the clear dividing line which they drew between themselves and their surrounding culture. Observance of the Torah, the Jewish law, especially relating to such obvious social markers as food laws and sabbath observance, gave their community cohesion and a clear boundary.

Marriage was permitted only within the community. Before the fall of Jerusalem and the ensuing exile, Israelites may have been more easy-going about choosing marriage partners from outside their community. Ruth the Moabitess, who was to be king David's great grandmother, was one example of easy acceptance of a foreign woman into an Israelite community. While the people were secure in possession of the land, it was no threat to their identity to take women from other communities into their midst. But when the community was being rebuilt after the exile in Babylon, the atmosphere had changed radically. Ezra and Nehemiah, who led reform and renewal of the returned exiles in Jerusalem in the fifth century BC, were vehement in forbidding marriage to 'outsiders'. One of the cornerstones of their reforming policies was to break up such unions, and insist on marriage within the community of Israel only (Ezr. 9–10, Neh. 10:30; 13:23–31). The aim of this policy was to secure offspring who belonged fully and without any ambiguity to the covenant people, a 'holy race' as they are described in Ezra 9:2. In the Jewish culture of the first century, therefore, children had great importance in assuring the future of the community. Children conceived within purely Jewish marriages, and brought up strictly within the ancestral tradition, guaranteed a future for a community whose survival depended on loyalty to their covenant faith. It was such a childhood and upbringing that Paul recalled in his letter to the Philippians: 'Circumcised on my eighth day, Israelite by race, of the tribe of Benjamin, a Hebrew born and bred', (Phil.3:5). Many Jewish men could recall a childhood like this with satisfaction.

Children had always, of course been the seed of the future. In an agrarian society, the well-being of the family depended on children, male children especially, to grow up and eventually take over the family holding. Fertility was a principal concern. Childlessness was more than a personal sorrow; it was a cause of 'shame', of loss of face in the community. The first reaction of Elizabeth, the mother of John the Baptist, to her pregnancy was a sense that the Lord had taken away her shame (Lk.1:25). Conversely, having a large number of children, especially sons, built up the honour of the family. The writer of Psalm 127 rejoiced in the prospect of a family well supplied by God with sons:

Sons are a gift from the Lord and children a reward from him. Like arrows in the hand of a warrior are the sons of one's youth. Happy is he who has his quiver full of them; someone like that will not have to back down (lit. 'they will not be ashamed') when confronted by an enemy in court. (Psalm 127:3-5)

Family continuity was so vital that Hebrew law contained provisions to ensure that a man's 'name' would continue, even if he died without children. The so-called 'levirate law' (from the Latin *levir*, a brother-in-law) obliged an Israelite to marry his sister-in-law if his brother should die childless (Deut.25:5f.). The children of this second marriage would be regarded as the heirs and successors of the dead brother or kinsman. It was quite possible that a man might be unwilling to do this. On the only occasions where we can see this custom or law operating in the Old Testament, the nearest kinsman was reluctant to do what was required (Gen.38:8–10, Ruth 4:1–6). In the case of Ruth, we learn that the kinsman would not take the widow for fear that his own inheritance might be jeopardized (Ruth 4:6). The law foresaw this possibility, and invoked the powerful sanction of public shaming to force the kinsman to do that which the honour of his family required of him (Deut.25:7–10).

The strong emphasis on fertility and procreation is common to peasant communities the world over. Indeed, the promise of fertility was one of the main lures of the cult of Baal, against which the prophets of the pre-exilic period had struggled so vehemently.

What distinguished Jewish attitudes in the New Testament period was that they added to this basic concern with procreation a strong emphasis on purity of marriage (choosing marriage partners only within the covenant people), and an equally strong emphasis on the careful education and upbringing of children born within the covenant. It was important that children should be a 'holy race'; not only born from a 'holy' union, but growing up to follow in the way of their parents.

There were some ascetic groups within the Judaism of the New Testament period. They rejected marriage and enjoined celibacy on their members. Such were the main part of the Essenes, whose commitment to celibacy we learn about from the first-century Jewish historian Josephus (*Wars* 2.8.2), and who were perhaps the group which produced the Dead Sea Scrolls. But even they, who did not permit their own members to marry, recognized that the continuance of the race depended on procreation and took care to bring children into their communities, to be brought up according to their own way of life. One might have expected that such an ascetic group would have had no place for children. But they shared the common Jewish perception that children and their education were of value and importance.

Education in the Jewish Community

Like children everywhere, Jewish children in Judaea, Galilee and beyond had to learn the work that they were to follow when grown up. Girls had to learn to manage the household. Boys had to learn the work of their fathers, whether in the fields or in a trade. The school of the first-century rabbi, Hillel, taught that negotiations for a son's apprenticeship had the same status as teaching him the scriptures; both could be done on a sabbath (*Babylonian Talmud, Shabbath 12a*). Education beyond induction into a trade had a special and honoured place within Judaism. To secure the future of the Jewish community, it was not enough to have children. They had to be brought up in the ancestral faith. It was the proud and justifiable boast of the Jews that their education of the young was unsurpassed in its thoroughness and comprehensiveness. Josephus, in his work *Against Apion*, pointed to the honoured place of the Law of Moses as the foundation and basis for Jewish education. Children could not be neglected, because:

> It [the Law] orders that they shall be taught to read, and shall learn both the laws and the deeds of their forefathers, in order that they may imitate the latter, and, being grounded in the former, may neither transgress nor have any excuse for being ignorant of them. (Josephus, *Against Apion* 2.25.204)

The goal of Jewish education was the practice of the Law. To reach that goal meant, in the first place, mastery of biblical Hebrew, which was not the language of everyday life in the Jewish community. Next it was necessary to read the Scriptures. Reading the Scriptures included committing large portions to memory. It seems likely that memorizing was a large part of the educational process. Beyond reading and memorizing the Scriptures, would come the task of understanding the comments and explanations of the teachers of the Law. These scholarly explanations made the text relevant to the present day and its preoccupations. Such study of the Torah was no antiquarian quest, but a means of leading the child in the intensely practical path of obedience to the Law. The twin accomplishments of memorizing and understanding were the two at which Josephus claimed he had excelled during his schooldays (*Life* 8(2)). Later rabbinical scholars wrote of 'the chirping of children' as the typical noise to be heard from a schoolroom where children were chanting their lessons (Safrai 1976 953).

Jewish education, therefore, aimed not just to develop knowledge or even understanding, but knowledge and understanding applied to daily living.

In previous ages, formal education seems to have been exclusively the task of the father of the family. But by the first century, Jewish parents had schools available where reading and the Torah were taught. Writing seems to have been regarded as a separate skill. To be able to write was not necessary to study the Scriptures, and although many Jews acquired this ability it was more by way of an additional professional accomplishment. Luke's birth narrative accurately reflects this Jewish educational gap between reading and writing: Zechariah could write the simple words, 'His name is John', but was apparently unable to write the story of his encounter in the temple and had to rely on signs (Lk. 1:22,63). Rabbinic tradition ascribed the first founding of schools to Simeon ben Shetah, who enjoined, around 100 BC, that children be sent to school. The Talmud identifies Joshua ben Gamla as particularly prominent in the setting up of a comprehensive system of education around the start of the first century AD. The tradition enshrined in the Talmud states that before the time of ben Gamla there had been some instruction for youths from the age of sixteen or seventeen, but they had proved too independent and not amenable to discipline. Ben Gamla therefore took the step of organizing the appointment of teachers in each town, to provide schooling for boys from the age of six or seven (Safrai 1976 947f.).

It may well be that these synagogue schools were set up in order to counter the attraction of Greek education, which, like other aspects of Greek civilization, had the potential to win Jews away from observance of their laws and customs. The Hellenization of culture around the eastern Mediterranean had been proceeding since the time of Alexander in the fourth century BC and by the time of the New Testament, Greek culture dominated the region. Many indigenous peoples embraced Hellenism with enthusiasm, but from the outset Jews resisted the polytheistic culture which the conquering Greeks had brought with them.

Despite the cultural, religious, and sometimes military clashes of Greek and Hebrew, some Jews grew up to be at home in both cultural contexts. The philosopher Philo in Alexandria, for instance, was well versed in Greek philosophy, as well as in the religion of his ancestors. The historian Josephus collaborated with the Romans and wrote massive histories of the Jewish people in Greek, although he admitted that he wrote *The Jewish War* in Aramaic, and needed help to polish his Greek style. A 'Hebrew of Hebrews' like St.Paul could write in fluent colloquial Greek. Paul cites the Greek poet Menander in 1 Corinthians 15:33; he is credited with a quotation from Epimenides in Titus 1:12 and Luke credits him with a quotation from the poet Aratus in Acts 17:28. It is most likely that Paul should have carried tags from the poets in his memory from the days of his schooling. The provision of Hebrew education did not prevent Jewish parents from seeing the advantages for their children of acquiring Greek, the common language of the peoples of the Mediterranean. They would not have wanted to encourage disloyalty to their covenant faith, but anyone who intended to leave their home town was likely to need the Greek language. The linguistic pattern of Palestine (and probably of other areas) was highly complex, and bi- and tri-lingualism seem to have been common (Wise 1992 434-444).

All that has been said so far applies to boys and their education. Girls were not expected to learn to read and write, nor to engage in study of the Law. They no doubt acquired the skills they would need for their place in life from their mothers and other female relatives. But that place was restricted to the confines of the home. Their activities outside the home tended to be extensions of housework, such as shopping or drawing water (Safrai 1976 752). Male and female roles were strictly demarcated, and girls were being brought up for a very different life from their brothers.

A later rabbinic saying held that: 'He who teaches his daughter Torah teaches her extravagance' (*Sotah* 3:4). But that this was a point of view which could have been held in the first century is shown by a comment of Philo: 'The attitude of man is formed by reason, of woman by sensuality' (*De Opificio Mundi* 165). The education given to boys was not given to girls, not only because of their supposed inadequacies as pupils, but also (and this may be the reason for supposing them incapable of learning) because they were being prepared for a quite separate role in life.

Growing Up in the Jewish Community

Growing up, for a Jewish child, meant getting ready to take one's place in the family and in the religious community. For boys the first milestone in that process was circumcision on the eighth day, as prescribed by the Law. In the bitter struggle for national freedom in the second century BC, circumcision had become the supreme identifying mark of the covenant community (1 Macc. 1.60f.). The rite of circumcision was a vital ceremony in a boy's life.

The circumcision was a time of rejoicing for the family, and as we saw earlier, the fact that it was delayed for a week meant that the child had already survived the dangerous perinatal period. Luke states that the circumcision was also a naming ceremony (Lk. 1:59; 2:21). There is no contemporary Jewish evidence for this, and certainly in earlier times names were given at birth (Gen. 35:18; 1 Sam. 1:20). But it is likely that Jewish custom had been influenced by the Greek practice of giving a name several days after the birth, and quite probably the ceremony of circumcision had attracted this additional dimension by the first century. Birthdays, incidentally, must have been noted, as so many stages of life depended on knowing one's age. But in pious households birthdays were not annual celebrations: in the Bible as a whole, only Pharaoh and Herod are recorded as celebrating their birthdays!

The choice of a name was important and was more than merely the search for a name which sounded attractive to the parents. In the early period of Israel's history, the name often took the form of an omen for the child's future life. In the Old Testament, in many instances, the mothers named the child, and it was assumed that the name would bear a relation to the child's circumstances. Leah and Rachel, for instance, named Jacob's sons (Gen. 29:32, 30:24) with names which were related to the circumstances of their birth. It was Samuel's mother, Hannah, who gave him his name (1 Sam. 1:20). In the book of Ruth the women of the neighbourhood chose a name for Ruth's son (Ruth 4:17).

Even if women usually chose names for their children, fathers were still expected to reject unsuitable names, or ones which were ill-omened. So, when the dying Rachel called her last child 'Ben-Oni' ('son of my sorrow'), Jacob renamed him 'Ben-jamin' or 'son of the right hand' - the right side being the well-omened side of the body (Gen. 35:18). David chose the royal or throne name of his son Solomon ('Peace'), and under prophetic guidance gave him the name Jedidiah ('Beloved by the Lord': 2 Sam.12.24f.). Politically sensitive names such as those for the king's sons may well have been dictated by the royal advisors and seers.

By the first century of the Christian era, the choice of names seems to have been directed by other considerations. In Luke's gospel we have the scene of John the Baptist's naming (Lk. 1:58–64). As with Ruth and her son, the friends and neighbours appear to have chosen the name. The name they favoured was his father's name: Zechariah. But John's mother, Elizabeth, was not willing to accept the name and insisted on the name given to the child by the angel: John. As with Jacob and Benjamin, the father was the ultimate court of appeal; his naming of the child was final. The neighbours' objection to the name John is significant. There was nothing intrinsically wrong with it, but, they said, 'There is nobody in your family who has that name'. The fact that a name would normally be chosen from an existing 'pool' of family names indicates again the strength of the bonds of lineage and descent which helped mark out the Jewish community.

The process of education and socialization has already been referred to under education. The end result of this process was emergence into adulthood, marked (for boys) by taking on the 'yoke of the Torah' at thirteen, and (for both sexes) by marriage; probably at some point in the mid teens. We know a little about how boys were prepared for adulthood, but we know virtually nothing about how girls were prepared for their adult life. This is because boys emerged into the public life of politics and religion, of which details can be found in the surviving literature. But girls were confined, in general, to the private world of the domestic sphere, of which the details were never committed to writing, and have therefore been lost to us. We can say that the main goal of a girl's parents was that she should enter marriage, and enter it both as a virgin, which was essential, and as a competent household manager, which was desirable. The limits of her way of life, and the content of her upbringing, will have been defined by these demands and expectations.

Initiation into the rituals and practices of the ancestral ways began very early on for the young Jewish boy, and first-century rabbis reminded fathers that the duty of observing Torah was to be introduced in childhood. The two rival rabbis, Hillel and Shammai, put it in this typically vivid way: Hillel said that a boy who could take his father's hand and walk to the Temple hill was obliged to keep the major feasts, while Shammai, not to be outdone, said the obligation began when a boy could ride there on his father's shoulders (Strack-Billerbeck 2, 146).

Children were participants in the home-based worship of Judaism, as well as being encouraged to observe the Temple-based rites. At Passover, the children were to ask the important questions which elicited, year by year, the explanation for the Passover ritual (Exod. 12:26f.). A gradual course of initiation is suggested by the following saying, which comes from a period later than the first century, but no doubt reflects a sentiment which had guided Jewish parents for a long time: 'A minor who knows how to shake a *lulav* [palm branch] is obliged to observe the laws of the *lulav*; a minor who knows how to wrap himself in the *tallit* [prayer shawl] is obliged to observe the law of the *zizit* [threads on the corners of the *tallit*] (*Tosefta, Hagigah* 1.2).

So the boy's taking on the yoke of the Torah at thirteen was not something novel for which he was unprepared. It marked the point at which he assumed responsibility for his own observance of the Torah. And it marked, not the end of study of the Torah, but the beginning of adult study, reflection and observance.

Initiation into Torah observance was something which concerned boys only. Marriage concerned both sexes, and equally clearly demarcated a person's emergence from childhood. Rabbi Samuel the Younger (late first century) is recorded as saying that 'at eighteen [a man is fit for] the bridal chamber' (*Mishnah, PirkeAboth* 5.21). Marriage was an obligation, not an option, and was generally entered on at an early age. Not to marry was a possibility, but one so rarely taken as to excite comment. It was thought wise to marry young people off early so as to limit the possibility of sexual adventures, especially on the part of girls. Girls and women could bring shame on a family through their behaviour. Around 200 BC, Jesus ben Sirach wrote a book filled with advice for living. His work is found in the Apocrypha of Protestant Bibles (and among the Deuterocanonical works of Catholic Bibles) under the title Ecclesiasticus or the Wisdom of Sirach. He explained at length what a Jewish father of the time felt about daughters:

> A daughter is a secret anxiety to her father,
> and worry about her keeps him awake at night;
> when she is young, for fear she may grow too old to marry,
> and when she is married, for fear her husband may divorce her;
> when she is a virgin for fear she may be seduced
> and become pregnant in her father's house;
> when she has a husband, for fear she prove unfaithful,
> and after marriage, for fear she may be barren.
> Keep close watch over a headstrong daughter,
> or she may give your enemies cause to gloat,
> making you the talk of the town, a byword among the people,
> shaming you in the eyes of the world.
> Give her a bedroom without windows,
> a room that does not overlook the entrance.
> Do not let her display her beauty to any man,
> or sit gossiping in the women's quarters;
> for out of clothes comes the moth,
> and out of woman comes woman's wickedness.
> Better a man's wickedness than a woman's goodness;
> it is woman who brings shame and disgrace.
>   (Ecclesiasticus 42.9-14)

The same author put his worries about adolescent daughters more succinctly in 7.24: 'Have you daughters? Keep a close watch over them' (lit. 'Give heed to their body'). A marriage arranged by the parents, probably well before their daughter's puberty and entered into quite soon after its onset, was the usual answer to these worries. Although, if ben Sirach is to be believed, the anxious father was then only exchanging one set of concerns for another. Even in the house of her husband a daughter could bring shame and disgrace on her parents by failing in one way or another to fulfil the role expected of her. No wonder ben Sirach concluded gloomily that: 'the birth of a daughter means loss' (Ecclus.22.3).

We should not suppose that every family was run on the stern lines that a moralist such as ben Sirach laid down. But he was trying to show how to avoid shame, a major motivating fear in the society of the time. Early marriage was a prudent course which most parents no doubt tried to follow, if possible, because then the choice of partner and the time of marriage was their decision and not the decision of the couple concerned. Arranged marriages were the norm. Because marriage was the alliance of two families, as well as the union of the individuals, it was not just a personal matter between the individuals, but a decision to be made by the families concerned. It involved intangible considerations such as family honour, as well as tangible ones such as payment of dowry.

Children in the Gentile World

Life in the Jewish community was diverse in many details, but had a certain homogeneity, centred as it was around the scriptures and the traditions of the Jewish people. On the other side of the cultural and religious divide, in the Gentile world, life was altogether more diverse.

Of Gentiles in the first century of the Christian era, we are probably best informed about well-to-do people in Rome, as this group has left the most abundant materials. But the religious assumptions of such people, their financial means and consequent access to education, together with their expectations for their children's future, would have been very different from those of, for example, slaves in provincial cities or peasant farmers in remoter parts of the countryside. So we must be aware that what we know about the group at the heart of imperial power and the impression they give us, is not a complete picture of how all inhabitants of the Roman Empire regarded their children and brought them up.

Children in the Gentile Family

Children occupied a more ambiguous position in Gentile society, generally, than in the Jewish community. Jewish children were the guarantee of the future for a community which knew itself to be always only one generation away from extinction. Gentile societies too recognized that children were the seed of the future, but did not always have such an unqualified positive attitude to children as their Jewish contemporaries.

Children were marginal figures in the society of the ancient world.

The central and key figure was the free adult male, able to bear arms and play his part in the religious, military and political life of the community. Women, children and slaves were peripheral figures. They found their place in society around and in dependence on the free adult males. The marginal position of the child was underlined by the Roman custom of burying infants who had died at less than forty days of age under the threshold of a house, or beneath the foundations of its walls (Wiedemann 1989 179); it symbolically put the child on the edge of the household.

As has already been noted, at least some sections of Gentile society in the first century did not wish to have large families, or even families at all, if we are to judge from successive attempts by Roman rulers from the time of Julius Caesar to penalize celibacy and encourage childbearing among Roman citizens. It may well be that in some parts of the Empire families were large, but in Rome families were usually small, and two or three surviving children (which often meant several more did not survive childhood) was the normal pattern (Rawson 1986 8).

A well-to-do Roman household would have been larger than the nuclear family of parents and natural offspring. It would have included slaves and, quite probably, foster-children or children adopted by the father. Adoption was of great importance in Roman law and society.

The father of the household, or *paterfamilias*, was the oldest surviving male ascendant. Traditionally in Roman law he had power of life and death over the members of the family. Although this power was not exercised by the first century of the Christian era with the exception of the decision to expose a newborn infant, the *paterfamilias* had huge authority which included full power over family property. The state did not interfere with his treatment of the women and children (including adult children) of his household.

This picture of an all-powerful *paterfamilias* should be qualified by two observations. One is that the father of the family would normally seek the opinions and guidance of a family council before major decisions. He was potentially an autocrat, but in practice usually exercised his powers with the consent of those under his authority. The other observation is that most men did not live long: a man's average life expectancy has been estimated as twenty-two years. It would be a fortunate man who lived to see his grandchildren grow up, and many fathers must have died while their children were still in infancy. We have to imagine that, even if in theory Roman society was made up of households, each of which was a small kingdom ruled by its *paterfamilias*, in fact there would have been many households where a widowed mother was the head.

Such were the sorts of families and households into which Gentile children in the time of the New Testament were born.

Early Childhood

Stoic philosophers divided human life into seven ages. Childhood occupied the first two: from birth to the age of seven, when the principle of reason is not yet active; and from seven to fourteen, when the principle of reason or rationality is developing. This philosophical division was artificial, but not entirely arbitrary, as it corresponded in a rough way to the stages of growing up in the first-century world.

A baby's entry into the family began with an inspection: a weakly infant, or one not wanted because of the family's poverty or the sex of the child, was likely to be exposed to die. It had not yet become a member of the family and had no name. Formal reception into the family circle was marked in Roman families by a simple ceremony in which the newborn infant was placed on the ground and then lifted up by the father (Augustine, *City of God*, 4.11; Suetonius, *Nero*, 6.1). The ground on which the baby was placed may have been thought to imbue him or her with the power of growth which comes from mother earth. (It was also the Roman custom to lay a corpse on the ground, perhaps with the thought of its life-force returning to the earth.) The father's taking the child in his arms symbolized very clearly the child's acceptance into the family.

Naming the child was postponed until the end of the first week of life. Many children succumbed to illness in those early days of life, and, as was noted earlier, post-natal mortality was high. But those who survived the first week were given their names in the celebration of the *dies lustricus*–'day of purification'–which for boys came on the ninth day of life, and for girls on the eighth day. They were ceremonially washed, sacrifices were made on their behalf, and names were conferred on them (Macrobius, *Satires* 1.16.36). From that point onwards they became full members of the family. This entry into life of a Roman baby is described in Rawson 1991 10-15.

But what happened to those children who were not accepted into the family, the children who were exposed? Many, no doubt, died; some were rescued. There seem to have been accepted points in the cities of the ancient world where exposed children were left – frequently on rubbish tips or dung heaps. Passers-by who found them were at liberty to take them and bring them up, if they chose. They had power to decide whether these children were to be brought up as slaves or free. Such abandoned children had no protection from exploitation and abuse, and many would end up as slaves, prostitutes, or gladiators. Our sources say little directly about the exposure of newborn children. Was their silence evidence of total indifference, or of an uneasy conscience? When Philo wrote a polemical attack on the practice of exposure of infants (*Special Laws* 3.110-119, see above, p.4f.) he addressed his remarks to Gentiles and accused them of murder. Was he touching a sensitive point in the conscience of his Gentile neighbours?

It sometimes happened that exposed children grew up to have reasonably stable lives. In the second century Hermas, the Christian author of a vision known as *The Shepherd*, seems to have been a foundling brought up as a slave in a wealthy lady's household. But despite these occasional happy endings, the death of untold numbers of exposed infants and the wretched lives of so many who survived the ordeal, were the grisly realities which accompanied the glittering civilizations of Greece and Rome. The fact that the practice of exposure continued for centuries, tacitly sanctioned although not officially encouraged, reminds us of the different estimation of human life, and of infant life especially, which Judaism and Christianity brought to the ancient world.

To return to the life of the child who had survived the natural and human hazards of early infancy: the child under about seven years of age seems to have been mainly confined to the home and its occupations. If the family was a wealthy one, the child would expect to have a nurse. Many women of the poorer sections of society would take on the role of wet nurse to children in richer households. Roman women who could afford to do so preferred to abandon breast feeding, and handed their children over to wet nurses as soon as possible. The choice of an appropriate nurse - strong, vigorous, and healthy - was a topic on which medical writers of the ancient world offered quantities of advice to mothers. They also recommended swathing or swaddling as a necessary part of bringing up a baby. Swathing kept a baby docile, of course, but the ostensible reason for the practice was as a way of shaping the child's body. The swathing which doctors recommended was prolonged and restricting. Nurses appear to have disagreed, and allowed babies more freedom, especially for the child's legs. Doctors thought that nurses simply wanted an easy life, and to be spared the chore of changing soiled swathing bands so frequently. Here is one example of a conflict between male theorists and female practioners which no doubt happened in other areas of child-rearing, too. If we had sources written by the nurses, telling us what they did, rather than by the doctors, telling us what the nurses and mothers ought to have done, then our picture of child care in the ancient world might have been rather different.

However, even the more lenient swathing regime of the nurse would seem a hard one to us today. Our custom of allowing children freedom of movement from the earliest age is the exact opposite of the custom of the ancient world. They set themselves to mould the child, physically as well as in behaviour, from the start of its life (Rousselle 1988 52-7). We can only speculate as to the psychological effect of swathing, with its long periods of restriction followed by brief times of release and freedom.

Weaning could be expected at around eighteen months to two years. One of the most respected of medical writers, Galen (fl. c.150), could write of this period as the start of the time when the child would be 'old enough to understand blows and threats'. We must suppose that a tough disciplinary regime would be experienced by children from a very young age. Even in the ancient world, though, there were voices raised in protest at the prevailing brutality of child-rearing, such as that of Athenaeus, another medical writer (early first century AD), whose enlightened view was that: 'Small children who have just been weaned should be allowed to play and do as they please' (Galen and Athenaeus cited in Rousselle 1988 58).

A little later, the child might be put into the charge of a male childminder. The Romans gave such men the title of *paedagogus*, a word they had borrowed from the Greeks, meaning 'one who leads a boy'. The Romans borrowed not only the word and the concept, but the personnel too, as many *paedagogi* were Greek slaves. The work of the *paedagogus* was to attend to the child, especially taking the child to school, and overseeing his conduct while at school. Eventually the child would grow out of the need for this attendant's services. St.Paul used the figure of the *paedagogus*, well-known to his readers either from their own experience, or as a familiar sight of the streets, to explain to the Galatian churches the relationship of the Law of the Old Testament to the Christian: 'The Law was our *paedagogus* to bring us to Christ, so that by faith we might be declared justified; and now that faith has come, we are no longer under a *paedagogus*' (Gal. 3:24f.: author's translation). Like the slave who cared for a young child and accompanied him until he was ready to move on to his eventual schoolmaster, the Law of the Old Testament had its proper function, but a limited one.

Bonds between children and these early childhood carers could be strong, and nurses were sometimes recalled with great affection by adults in later life. The younger Pliny made generous financial provision for his nurse when she had grown old (*Letters* 6.3).

Children would not gain any formal education from their nurses and *paedagogi*; this was not their role. But undoubtedly they learned much from their early carers, probably encountering the rich store of popular fables and legends in the stories their nurses would tell to amuse and entertain their charges - or to frighten them into good behaviour. If their *paedagogus* happened to be Greek, as many of them were, the child might well acquire a facility with the Greek language as a bonus from the time spent in his company.

Children also played. Their toys were simple, and those discovered by archaeology are often ones which imitate adult life, such as small carts or tools. Balls were always popular as toys. Dolls, too, made frequent appearances as toys, but dolls in antiquity were not models of babies. They were based on models of young women. A point was being made: girls were being prepared for their role as wives and household managers, and their chosen toys were already making them ready for that role.

Few people in the ancient world seem to have given much attention to children's play or to have understood its importance. One exception was the Roman educator, Quintilian, who wrote the first systematic treatise on education to have survived. He accepted that learning for the child should include elements of play, and indeed, that play is learning. He saw that children's games, such as asking one another riddles, contributed to the learning process (*Inst.Or.* 1.3.11). Quintilian advocated, for instance, that young children learning the alphabet be given cut-outs of the various letters to familiarize them with the shapes (*Inst.Or.* 1.1.26). This was a huge advance on the conventional pattern of setting children first to learn the names of letters and their order before they were shown what they looked like - and, for Roman children, to learn the Greek alphabet before the Latin one, on the assumption that Latin would be easy by contrast!

School Age

The work of Quintilian brings us to the second period of the child's life, that beginning at seven, when the principle of reason or rationality was thought to be forming in the child. Quintilian proposed formal education to begin before the seventh year, but custom had established this as the appropriate beginning of the educational process.

The level of education available for a child varied according to status, means and location. Many adults who appear in the papyri from Egypt, one of our best windows on the life of working people in the ancient world, were evidently illiterate. But in Pompeii, the city overwhelmed by the eruption of Vesuvius in 79 AD, the abundant graffiti preserved on the walls show that many townsfolk of quite humble origins were able to read and write. The Roman army could function only on the basis of a widespread literacy which would enable its administrative work to carry on. So we should suppose that most free people of any means would secure for their children at least a basic competence in reading, writing and, in all probability, numeracy. Even many slaves achieved some competence in these. Pliny the Younger liked to have (and liked his friends to know that he had) both freedmen, such as Zosimus, and slaves, such as Encolpius, who could read and declaim for him (*Letters* 5.19, 8.1). Pliny's literate slaves were far from unique, as witnessed by the advice of a writer on farming; that slaves in a position of responsibility on a farm should be able to read, write, and handle accounts (Varro, *Rerum rusticarum* 1.17.4). Slaves with such accomplishments must have been available. And we have the undeniable fact that many schoolteachers were slaves or freedmen. So literacy in the first century AD, though not universal, stretched far down the social scale, and we must therefore assume that schooling of some form was part of the childhood experience of many inhabitants of the Empire.

As in Jewish society, the original ideal of the Romans was that each child should be taught what they needed to know and understand by their parents, and the place of the father as his son's instructor was highly valued by conservatively-minded Romans. In his fourteenth *Satire*, the Roman satirist Juvenal heavily laboured the theme of parental influence for good and ill, and, incidentally, testified to the success of the Jewish community in passing on its laws and manners within the family from generation to generation – even though he considered their customs pernicious (Juvenal, *Satires* 14.96-106).

By the first century BC, both Romans and Jews were experiencing the strong attractions of an alternative form of education: the Greek model. It took education out of the home and placed it in a new institution, the school. The role of the father as his son's instructor was an aspect of both Roman and Jewish cultures which contrasted strongly with Greek society. A Greek father who spent too much time with his children, away from the 'proper' companionship of other men, risked ridicule (Marrou 1965 344).

In a simple society, and among leisured people, traditional methods might work well enough. Fathers could pass on to their sons their own skills and accomplishments, as well as teaching them to swim, box and so on. No doubt this was also the work of mothers who shared their domestic skills with their daughters. But as Roman society became more complex, and as Romans became aware of the greater sophistication of Greek thought and culture, it became a matter of increasing necessity to hand a large part of formal education over to professional schoolteachers. While the Jewish community established its own distinctive pattern of synagogue-based schooling, Roman society adopted largely Greek methods of education.

The pattern of elementary schooling, which occupied the years from about seven to fourteen, had become established in the cities of the Greek world, and from there spread to Rome. But in New Testament times, access to schools may have been limited to those living in large cities, both in the Greek East and in the Latin West (Kleijwegt 1991 76-83).

Those families whose means and location gave them access to education would have ensured that at around seven years of age, their children were sent to the school of the teacher, known in Greek as a *grammatistes*, and in Latin as a *litterator*. Under their supervision, children would learn the basic skills of reading, writing, and reckoning. The teacher would rent a room, or even space in the street under an awning, and hold his classes there. The school day was long, methods generally unimaginative, and discipline sometimes brutal. The stick or the switch were the symbols of the schoolmaster's work, quite as much as the instruments of reading and writing. St Augustine wrote eloquently and perceptively about his memories of the violence meted out to him at school in *Confessions* 1.9. He recalled that his first prayers had been to be spared a beating at school, and that his parents had laughed at his sufferings. In his typically lucid way, he reflected that: 'We enjoyed playing games, and were punished for them by men who played games themselves' - for he noted that the competitive spirit which animated their children's play also drove his teachers to the parallel 'games' of ambition and argument.

Children would learn to form their letters, not on papyrus (which was expensive and could be used only a limited number of times), but on a waxed wooden tablet (like that mentioned by Luke in Lk. 1:63). Not only could the tablet be used and reused, as the wax was smoothed out after being marked with a stylus, but the teacher could rule lines on it, or make shallow impressions in the wax for the child to go over more firmly with their stylus. It is a school exercise such as this which 1 Peter refers to when it describes Christ as leaving us an 'example' to follow - the word used is *hypogrammos*, the outline in the wax for the pupil to copy (1 Pet. 2:21). Waxed tablets were still used for some purposes even in adult life, but the student who progressed would eventually practise their writing on papyrus, too, as is shown by some surviving papyri, which contain what are evidently school exercises. Writing on papyrus (or boards, which were also used) would be with a pen made of reed. Desks do not seem to have been used, and pupils wrote with their tablets on their knees.

Some aspects of ancient educational practice strike us as misdirected. It has already been said that Latin-speaking children had to learn the Greek alphabet first. Not only was this the case, but the unfortunate children had to learn the names of the Greek alphabet forwards and backwards before they were even allowed to look at the shapes of the letters! Some contemporaries recognized the absurdity of this approach (Quintilian, *Inst.Or.*1.0.1, 1.2.6; Jerome, *Letters* 107.4.2).

Having learned the names of the letters, the pupil would practise writing them, then move on to writing combinations of letters, and after that whole words. The pupil's copybook sentences for the next stage would be drawn from morally uplifting sentiments, or quotations from the poets. Roman children would learn the contents of the Twelve Tables, which were the basis of Roman law and customs.

Numbers were more difficult. Both Greek and Latin used letters to denote numerical values, and both systems were harder to compute with than our present-day system of Arabic notation. They also lacked a zero, which compounded the difficulties for mathematicians in the ancient world. Children acquired a basic numeracy, but the prestige subjects in the ancient curriculum were literature and oratory, and this emphasis may have contributed to the relative neglect of mathematics.

We have a vivid picture of a day in the life of a schoolchild from a rather odd source: a series of phrase books, compiled in the early third century for Greek-speakers learning Latin, which have survived in a number of versions. These texts set out typical phrases one might need in various situations, and among the situations envisaged is a schoolchild's day. We remember that these are passages written by an adult, but no doubt the compilers of these phrase collections were drawing on their own experience of childhood. The following passage draws together material from two such exercises, the *Hermeneumata Stephani* Colloquy 2 (Goetz 1892 379-90) and the *Colloquia Monacensia* (Goetz 1892 644-7). (The sources are indicated as HS or CM.)

Early in the morning, when I had woken up, I got up and I called the slave. I told him to open the window. He opened it quickly. When I had got up I sat down on the side of the bed. I called for my shoes and socks, because it was cold (HS).

When I had my shoes on I took a towel. A clean one was given to me. Water was brought for my face in a pot. With it I washed first my hands, then my face, then inside my mouth. I rubbed my teeth and gums. I spat out what was not needed as it was left over, and I blew my nose. All these things were thrown away. I dried my hands, then my arms and my face, so that I might go out clean. Because that is how a free-born boy should learn (HS).

I laid down the counterpane, put on a tunic, put a belt round me, I put oil on my hair and combed it. I made a coil of scarf around my neck. I put on my white overtunic and a cloak over everything. (CM)

I went out of the bedroom with the paedagogus and with the nurse to greet my father and mother. I greeted them both and I was kissed.(CM)

Then I looked for my stylus and my notebook, and these I handed to my slave. With everything ready, I went out with a good omen and followed by my paedagogus went straight through the door which leads to school(HS).

Some of my friends came to meet me. I greeted them and they greeted me back (HS).

So I came to the stair. I went up the steps calmly, as it is right to, and in the vestibule I took off my cloak and I combed my hair. And so having come upstairs I went into the middle room (HS).

I went in and I said 'Greetings, sir'. He kissed me and returned my greeting. My slave gave me my box of writing tablets, my case of styli, and my ruler. When I have sat down I smooth out my place [on the waxed tablet] (CM).

I do my writing beside the examples to copy. When I have written, I show my work to the teacher. He corrects it and erases it. He orders me to read (CM).

[An older child describes his work] So I went into my place, I sat down, I held out my right hand, I lowered my left hand to my clothes. And so I began to recite as I had received the things to be learned (HS).

When we have done these things, the teacher lets us go for lunch. Leaving school, I go home. I change, and I have white bread, olives, cheese, dried figs and nuts. I drink some cold water. When I have eaten I return again to school. I find the teacher reading out, and he said: 'Begin from the beginning' (CM).

Several interesting points emerge in this phrase book from antiquity. The place of the *paedagogus* in the child's life is shown very clearly, and it is of interest that the nurse continued to have a place in the child's routine even after he had reached school age. An omen was taken before leaving the house - a reminder of the everyday place of religion and ritual in children's lives. The children described here are, of course, models of behaviour, and show us the attention to hygiene and to decorous behaviour which a small boy was expected to exhibit. We may well wonder whether in practice children behaved quite as perfectly as these examples!

In school, we are made aware of the repetitive and rather dull work which the child is set to do. The younger pupil still learning his letters is given *hypogrammata* (examples) to copy. These may have been the moral precepts mentioned previously, or perhaps short phrases equivalent to our 'The quick brown fox jumps over the lazy dog': brief texts which contained all the letters of the alphabet. Three such *hypogrammata* are known in Greek. Literacy and literary studies were the main staple of the children's day, though their writing exercises both at the early and the later stages were punctuated by sessions of reading aloud to the teacher. The teacher was evidently checking on progress, as is witnessed by his correction of the writing exercise. He also prepared his pupils for public speaking. The older pupil carefully takes up an orator's posture before reciting his lesson. Not every child would become an orator, but rhetoric and its application to advocacy were the pinnacles of educational attainment. That goal of the process must have had its effect on shaping the lower stages of educational work.

And finally, we gain a delightful glimpse into the everyday moments of a child's life. We see something of the child's contact with the significant adults around him: *paedagogus*, nurse, parents, teachers. The phrase book writers wisely set their narrative in the winter, giving opportunity for longer descriptions of getting dressed. The school day was a long one. The *Colloquia Monacensia* describes it as beginning 'before dawn'. But it was broken up by lunch time, long enough to allow the pupil to go home for his frugal but healthy midday meal.

Later Childhood

At around twelve years of age, the pupil was expected to pass from the litterator to the more advanced work supervised by the *grammaticus*. With this second teacher he would pass from elementary literacy to the study of literature. Cicero, in the first century BC, set out a splendid picture of the curriculum to be followed at this stage of the child's education:

> In music, rhythms, sounds, and measures; in geometry, lines, figures, dimensions and magnitudes; in astronomy, the revolution of the sky, the rising, setting and movement of heavenly bodies; in literature, the study of poets, the learning of histories, the explanation of words and proper intonation in speaking them; and...the theory of oratory, invention, style, arrangement, memory and delivery. (*De Oratore*, 1.187).

But this picture was probably more an aspiration to be aimed at than a sober description of the reality of education as children experienced it, and was inspired by the example of a long-past Greek ideal. In practice, the curriculum was moulded by the assumption that its aim was to produce orators, it was fixed on the study of a set corpus of literature, and it continued the rote learning and unimaginative dinning of facts with which children had become familiar at the hands of the *litterator*.

The major Greek philosophers had envisaged a wide-ranging process of education, which included physical exercise and 'music' - that is, study and practice of all arts related to the Muses. Quite probably, in many Greek cities, this wider education remained the ideal; and a second-century inscription from Thrace (N.Greece) gives some evidence for this, as a group of pupils recorded in it their gratitude to their teacher of geometry (Kleijwegt 1991 90). But the syllabus for Roman children was much narrower than the character-forming *paideia* of which the Greek philosophers had spoken. The elementary schooling process was tedious or even painful in its methods and narrowly unimaginative in its scope, but it at least produced a large number of people, across the social spectrum, who could read, write, and, after a fashion, handle figures.

Girls shared in this education to some extent. Around 300 BC the Athenian poet Menander had written disparagingly of female education:

> Teach a woman letters? A terrible mistake!
> Like feeding extra venom to a terrifying snake.
> (*Fragment 702K*, cited in Bowen 1972 77)

But things had changed a little by the time of the New Testament. In the Greek city-state of old, the respectable woman's place was entirely confined to the home. Men provided the state's warriors and were the participants in its democracy. By contrast, women in the Roman Empire of the first century AD had a wider sphere of potential employment and a greater freedom of movement. In the New Testament we meet women like Lydia, the cloth merchant of Thyatira in Asia Minor, whose work had taken her across the Aegean Sea to Philippi, and Prisca, apparently a partner with her husband Aquila in their tent-making business (Acts 16:14, 18:2f.). These women, and others like them around the Empire, must have received some degree of education in childhood. On the most northerly outpost of the Empire, Hadrian's Wall, numbers of writing-tablets (see above, p.26) have recently been recovered. Among them are items of correspondence between officers' wives, of whom at least one, Claudia Severa, seems to have written with her own hand, giving us tangible proof of literacy among at least some women in the Roman Empire (Bowman & Thomas 1994 256).

We do not know a great deal about girls' education. Sometimes their presence in schools is mentioned in passing by Roman writers: Martial (*Epigrams* 9.68) complains of the loud-voiced and early-rising schoolteacher who is 'hateful to boys *and girls*', and Juvenal writes of girls who have not *yet* learned their alphabet (*Satires* 14.20-9). Roman parents seem to have held their daughters in equal esteem with their sons, and the two sexes appear to have shared at least in the same elementary education (Rawson 1986 18,40).

The culmination of a young person's education would be to pass from the *grammaticus* to the *rhetor*. The rhetorical school would build on the foundations laid earlier and would aim to turn out a polished public speaker, with all the resources of literature to hand and commanding a style which would win over his hearers. This phase of education would begin at around fifteen or sixteen, and we must suppose that it was the preserve of the wealthiest élite, whose sons were being trained to take prominent places in public life (Laistner 1951 10-17; Marrou 1965 292-307).

Finally on the topic of education, we should not assume that all learning was bookish, merely because most of our sources are literary. There were practical crafts and skills to be acquired, too, and some of these called for specialist training. Among the papyri preserved in Egypt, we find some apprenticeship contracts which parents took out for their sons. In 66 AD, for example, Trypho of the village of Oxyrhynchus (from which a large number of papyri have come) put his son Thoönis in the hands of the weaver Ptolemaeus for a year's apprenticeship in the weaving trade. The contract reveals that Thoönis was a minor (under fourteen), and that the weaver Ptolemaeus was one of those illiterate artisans mentioned previously when we considered the extent of literacy: the scribe Zoilus had to write out not only the contract, but also Ptolemaeus' own name (Oxyrhynchus Papyrus 275).

Children and Abuse

We have already seen how the Jewish writer of Ecclesiasticus feared that a daughter might become involved in a sexual liaison (Ecclesiasticus 42.9-14). In a striking parallel which says much about the contrast between Jewish and Gentile society, Juvenal expressed the perils awaiting a handsome son: he might well, said the poet, become the victim of a homosexual seducer (perhaps with the parents' connivance), or attract the attentions of a powerful and predatory older woman (*Satires* 14.295-328).

How did the Gentile world of the first century regard the sexual abuse of children and young people?

In his *History of Childhood*, Lloyd de Mause put his view starkly: 'The child in antiquity lived his earliest years in an atmosphere of sexual abuse' (de Mause 1974 43). He gathered some apparently damning quotations from ancient sources to justify this bleak vision of childhood in the ancient world. But it is doubtful whether we can be as dogmatically certain about the extent of such abuse as de Mause claimed. After all, with all the information and techniques available in our contemporary society, it is hard enough to establish the facts of child abuse. Trying to piece together the historical jigsaw out of evidence from the ancient world leaves far more uncertain results.

Certainly, the acceptance in Greek society of sexual relations between men and boys was a facet of the Gentile world which particularly appalled the Jews. Traditionally-minded Romans, too, disliked Greek gymnastics with its naked contests and the pederasty which often went with it. The acceptance and, indeed, encouragement of sexual liaisons between men and boys had begun in the military ethos of the Greek city-states. It was seen as a means of reinforcing loyalty to one another within the ranks of the citizen army. When the Greek city ceased to be a military unit, on the assimilation of Greece into the Roman Empire, the same relationship of man and boy reemerged as the bond between teacher and pupil (Marrou 1965 61-70).

In Rome, some parts of society accepted this 'Greek love' as a part of life; others saw it as a token of national degeneracy. The Emperor Nero, for example, was a great enthusiast for all things Greek, and the games he put on in 60 AD included Greek style naked boxing. But Tacitus, the historian, in describing these games, expressed the disgust and contempt of old-fashioned Romans for the values Nero supported: 'foreign influences demoralize our young men into shirkers, gymnasts and perverts' (*Annals* 14.20).

Gentile society in the time of the New Testament was divided about 'Greek love'. In some quarters there was an easy acceptance; in others a deep abhorrence. Sometimes we can see the uncertainty in one vacillating individual. The anonymous writer whose work on *The Education of Children* has passed under Plutarch's name is cited by de Mause as advising fathers to allow their sons' suitors to engage in sexual activity with them (de Mause 1974 45). But the pseudo-Plutarch was in fact rather more ambiguous. He was in two minds about it, as he says himself (*Education* 15). On the one hand his advice to parents was that children should be kept away from corrupting influences. On the other, he was well aware of the Greek tradition of love affairs between men and boys, and of the great names of the past who have been associated with such affairs. His compromise was to admit those who are 'lovers of the soul' and forbid 'those whose desire is for mere outward beauty' (*Education* 15). It is an uneasy compromise, and the author clearly found himself in a quandary. The picture, at any rate, is not as straightforward as de Mause presented it.

Something similar could be said of de Mause's reference to Petronius portraying the rape of a seven-year-old girl, with women clapping round the bed (de Mause 1974 44f.). Petronius' book the *Satyricon* is not a simple description of social customs. It is a scabrous fictional tale of low-life in southern Italy in the time of Nero. Its central personalities are two highly doubtful characters and the young boyfriend they share. The narrative concerns their outrageous criminal adventures and bizarre sexual escapades. Perhaps it is an accurate reflection of lower-class life, and its incidents might have been everyday events. But more likely it was written for the titillation of Nero's court, of whom Petronius was a prominent luminary. The particular incident which de Mause singles out occurs in the course of one of the debauches which punctuate the book, when the main character's boyfriend and the girl are bundled into bed together. Here as always in his book, Petronius portrays the participants as willing – though that attitude, of course, has always been part of the psychological armoury of the abuser.

And some people were aware of abuse as a problem. Quintilian, sensitive as always to the neglect of children's needs during their education, was aware also of the possibilities of abuse which the brutality of current teaching methods presented:

> If inadequate care is taken in the choice of respectable governors and
> instructors, I blush to mention the shameful abuse which scoundrels
> sometimes make of their right to administer corporal punishment, or the
> opportunity not infrequently offered to others by the fear thus induced in
> the victims. I will not linger on this subject: it is enough if I have made
> my meaning clear. I will content myself with saying that children are
> helpless and easily victimised, and that therefore no-one should be given
> unlimited power over them. (Quintilian, *Inst.Or.* 1.3.17)

We begin to see just how hard it is to get at the truth about sexual abuse
in the ancient world. Acceptance of physical abuse of children or of
sexual encounters between adults and children was not as universal as
de Mause, for instance, suggested. But then we must recognize that
practices may go on without being condoned by society at large. As our
contemporary experience shows, and as Quintilian's humane words
remind us, the basic problems of child abuse as we know them today
were already clear to sympathetic observers in the ancient world.

Sexual abuse of children certainly happened in antiquity. That it was
widespread is made likely by three elements of ancient society. One was
the long-standing tradition of 'Greek love', which was not universally
accepted, but was at least so common as to make it quite certain that many
boys would have had sexual encounters with men in the course of their
childhood. The second was the institution of slavery. We have already
seen that many foundlings ended up as slaves. We may well suspect that
child prostitution was rife in a community where many girls, in particular,
were abandoned and in which slavery was a normal state of existence.
In this respect the abuse of children was merely one part of the more
general abuse of human beings represented by the slavery of the ancient
world. The third element of ancient society conducive to the abuse of
children was the low esteem in which children were held. The poet
Juvenal may have said: 'You owe the utmost reverence to a child'
(*Satires* 14.47), but there is little evidence in our sources that much
reverence or even respect was accorded to children in general, beyond
the care taken by some parents for their own offspring. A general sense
of concern for the well-being of children as a whole is something entirely
lacking in the Gentile world of the first century.

If we choose to look at the dark side of the treatment of children in the
ancient world, it is indeed a miserable picture of neglect and abuse which
we see. De Mause would have us believe it is the whole picture. But there
were loving parents and there were people, such as the pseudo-Plutarch,
anxious to protect their children (though not children in general) from

abusive relationships. The strange contradictions in the ancient world of attitudes to children are seen in the poet Martial, capable of writing the touching epitaph for Erotion quoted earlier. Yet, quite evidently from his poems, Martial was a man whom we would consider an abuser of children. Even if the sexual abuse of children was not as universal as de Mause suggested, we can see enough in our very fragmentary sources to realize that for many children the world of New Testament times was a dark one.

Coming Of Age in the Gentile World

The transition from childhood to adulthood was marked by a variety of rituals; these both looked forward to the new stage of life which was beginning, and back to the childhood which the young person was leaving.

So a girl, at her marriage, would dedicate her dolls to Venus, in a formal leave-taking of childhood (Wiedemann 1988 149). A boy, on coming of age, similarly dedicated to the *Lares* (the household gods) the amulet which he wore round his neck to provide magic protection (Persius, *Satires* 5.30-31).

For a boy there was also the positive, forward-looking element of rejoicing, as he prepared to take on the role of an adult citizen. Signs of puberty were welcomed and celebrated. A boy's first beard was shaved as a formal 'depositing of the beard' (*depositio barbae*), and the shavings would be kept in a domestic shrine. Sometimes this shaving took place in the early teens, but for others it was delayed into the early twenties (Carcopino 1956 179).

At some time between twelve and eighteen years of age, but most likely between fourteen and sixteen, a father would decide that his son was ready for the responsibilities of adulthood and take him, with a group of male friends, to be enrolled in the list of citizens (Rawson 1986 41).

Most impressive of all was the donning of the *toga pura*, the all-white toga of manhood, in place of the boy's *toga praetexta*, with its distinctive purple hem. This would happen traditionally at the feast of the *Liberalia* on March 17th, so that the cohort of boys of similar age would all celebrate their coming to manhood together (Seneca, *Letter* 4.2; Cicero, *Ad Att.* 5.20.9; Ovid, *Fasti* 3.777).

In Roman society, it seems to have been customary for marriage to be contracted rather later than we might expect - at least among the well-to-do who have left their records in inscriptions. The legal minimum for marriage was set by Roman law at twelve for girls and fourteen for boys, while the emperor Augustus set the minimum age of betrothal at ten. However, study of inscriptions reveals that a bride's age at her first marriage was unlikely to be below fifteen, and more likely to be in the late teens, while men married for the first time somewhat later, typically in their late twenties (Treggiari 1991 398-403). Wealthy Romans therefore would have normally had a large age difference at the time of marriage, though given the high rate of mortality many people would have also married for a second time after losing their first spouse. Among other classes and in other parts of the Empire there was probably a smaller age gap between bride and groom, and marriage was probably contracted earlier.

So, in some parts of Gentile society at least, there was no sudden transition from childhood to adulthood at puberty. Many girls remained unmarried until well after the onset of puberty. Equally, many young men, though wearing the man's toga, had not yet taken on the responsibility of marriage and were still completing their education and upbringing.

Children in the religions of the Gentile World

Children had a significant part in the religious life of many cults in the Roman world. Perhaps it was partly because of their marginal position, which fitted them to be intermediaries between the world of men and the world of the gods. Perhaps, too, it was because their supposed innocence equipped them for the role of intermediary. Children took an active part in the choirs which sang for the gods in the sanctuaries of which we hear in Asia Minor (Fox 1986 178f).

In the home we find that children also had religious roles to perform. For example it was the Roman custom that when the father of the family offered sacrifice during a meal, the children's part was to declare whether the household gods looked favourably on the sacrifice (Servius *ad Aen*. 1.730, cited in Wiedemann 1989 179). There were also rituals in the home which centred around children, such as the *dies lustricus* and the coming-of-age celebrations which have already been mentioned, and we have noted the schoolboy taking an omen before setting out from home.

In the Gentile family, as well as in the Jewish family, children were included in a variety of religious rites and functions. The early Christians, whether from a Jewish or a Gentile background, would have been very well used to the involvement of children in acts of worship and in various daily and seasonal rituals.

Summary

At the start of the chapter we noted some of the difficulties in the way of building a clear picture of children in the world of the New Testament. Inevitably, what has been said here has tended to concentrate on the wealthy and literate, because they have left the written sources. We may have been misled into thinking some things were normal practice in the raising of children, when they were nothing more than the proposals of a reforming theorist.

However, we have been able to begin to understand both the tenderness and the cruelty of the treatment of children in the ancient world. Parents clearly loved their children; but financial necessity might drive them to expose them to die. Parents wanted the best for their children; but because they thought of children as animals to be tamed, their methods of bringing them up were bound to be harsh. Children were valued; but in a society where slavery was an unquestioned reality, the exploitation and abuse of children was simply part of the wider exploitation of human beings of all ages.

We have seen that the Jewish community nurtured a higher view of infant life. It also put greater store by the education of its male young people.

The Christian church was to be launched among the Jews. It was also to embrace the Gentiles. When we look at the first Christians' treatment of children, we should look to see what they inherited from their Jewish family background, and what they incorporated from their Gentile cultural context. But before doing that, we need to look at what the followers of Jesus of Nazareth were to learn about children, not from their religious background or cultural context, but from their Master himself.

Chapter 2

Children in the Gospels

Children are surprisingly conspicuous in the gospel stories about Jesus' ministry. Surprisingly, because of the general tendency of people in the ancient world to overlook them. When Matthew recounted the miraculous feeding of the five thousand, he drew his story to a close with the comment: 'Some five thousand men shared in this meal, not counting the women and children' (Matt.14:21). 'Not counting the children' was a good summary of a widespread attitude. But children did count for something in the ministry of Jesus. Children occur in several of the healings in the gospels. They also have their place in the teaching of Jesus. We find that Jesus was an observer of children, using the words of a child's game in one of his incisive sayings (Matt.11:16–19). One of the distinctive features of Jesus' message and ministry was the significance he attributed to children.

Jesus' ministry took place in Palestine, against a predominantly Jewish background, and its context was broadly that of the Jewish culture sketched out in the previous chapter. But the writings of the New Testament, in both the gospels and letters, were addressed, mainly, to people outside Palestine, on the fringe of Jewish culture or even outside it altogether. The New Testament writings, then, come from a context which was broadly that of the Gentile culture depicted in the previous chapter.

Matthew, Mark, Luke and John had access to many stories and sayings of Jesus, and it is quite likely that they did not use all the material to hand in telling their stories (see Jn.21:25). They selected and ordered their material in order to bring out what they wanted to say about Jesus (see Lk.1:2f.). Each one of the four evangelists composed a unique portrait of Jesus. And each was concerned with the relevance of Jesus for his readers here and now. They were not antiquarians, chronicling events from the past merely for their own sake. Each writer had, as far as we can see, a passionate conviction about the continuing importance of Jesus for his readers.

So, when we read the gospels, we have to bear in mind that Matthew, Mark, Luke and John have selected and ordered their material with the needs of their own day and their own readers in mind. No doubt they left out some sayings and stories which they knew but which did not fit into the narrative they were writing (Luke includes a saying of Jesus in Acts 20:35 which he did not put into his gospel). There are patterns of teaching and narrative in their gospels which suggest that they have brought their materials into a particular order, so as to group, for instance, teaching on related topics together in one place (Matthew has collected a section on church life in Matt.18). While the gospel writers are writing about Jesus, they are speaking to their contemporaries. In reading what the gospels have to say about children in the ministry of Jesus, we have to keep this dual perspective in mind.

We begin our look at children in the gospels with the way the gospels deal with the childhood of Jesus himself

The Child Jesus

> And through all his wondrous childhood
> he would honour and obey,
> love, and watch the lowly maiden
> in whose gentle arms he lay;
> Christian children all must be
> mild, obedient, good as he.
>
> For he is our childhood's pattern,
> day by day like us he grew;
> he was little, weak and helpless,
> tears and smiles like us he knew;
> and he feeleth for our sadness,
> and he shareth in our gladness.

Cecil Frances Alexander

A candid reader of the gospels would have to say that Mrs Alexander allowed herself a fair amount of poetic licence in her popular Christmas carol 'Once in royal David's city'. The carol, simply but movingly, presents three scenes in the story of Jesus: his birth, his childhood, and his return. For the first and final scenes, Mrs Alexander was able to draw on images and phrases from the scriptures. But the central scene, the childhood of Jesus as described in the stanzas above, is mainly composed of skilfully embroidered guesswork. She has put together her picture largely from Luke's summaries of Jesus' early life in Luke 2:40 ('The child grew big and strong and full of wisdom; and God's favour was upon him') and 2:51f. ('He continued to be under their authority . . . As Jesus grew he advanced in wisdom and in favour with God and men'), and from the words of Hebrews 4:15 ('Ours is not a high priest unable to sympathize with our weaknesses').

What also strikes us about the carol is the way in which Mrs Alexander has put into her picture exactly those childhood virtues prized by her own Victorian culture. Her Jesus is mild, obedient and good; the sort of child who is 'seen and not heard', even though the one specific story we have about Jesus as a child shows him troubling his parents by taking a very independent course (Lk.2:41–51). The hymn illustrates the tendency of every age to read into the scriptures what we expect to find there.

Aspects of biography, ancient vs modern

Anyone who wishes, as Mrs Alexander did, to write about Jesus' childhood faces an immediate difficulty: the gospels tell us virtually nothing about Jesus' life between his birth and the start of his public ministry around the age of thirty. This is one of the features of the gospels which most puzzles and disappoints a modern reader, and calls for some explanation.

It would be unfair to say that people in the ancient world were uninterested in children. As we have seen in the previous chapter, there is ample evidence for the love of parents for their offspring, and for society's concern with its future members. But while people in the ancient world were interested in children, they were not so interested in childhood.

Developmental psychology has revolutionized the way we think about childhood. Modern people have been taught to see childhood as a time of formation and growth, a time when a person passes through certain crucial stages of development. The ancient world was simply not so reflective about childhood and did not see human personality in the same developmental way. People in the ancient world recognized that there were a number of skills which growing children had to acquire, such as walking, speech, and the manual or mental skills of reading and writing. But they would generally assume that personality and character were fixed from the outset, and that human growth merely gave that character the chance to express itself.

So there are a number of questions which we would have liked the gospels to answer for us about the child Jesus. What were the influences on him as he grew up? What degree of formal education did he acquire, and did he, for instance, attend a synagogue school of the sort mentioned in the last chapter? We assume that he grew up to speak Aramaic in the home (Jesus is quoted as speaking Aramaic in Mk.5:41), and it seems highly likely that he gained fluency in Hebrew, the language of the scriptures – in Luke 4 Jesus is shown reading the Hebrew scriptures in the synagogue, and throughout his ministry he discussed religious matters with the scribes, who held their debates in Hebrew (Wise 1992 442). But to what extent was he exposed to Greek, the language of trade? And what of Jesus' home life? Was Joseph still alive when he reached adulthood? Were the 'brothers' and 'sisters' mentioned in the gospels also sons of Mary (Mk.3:31, 6:3)? Or does 'brother' here mean 'cousin', as the Roman Catholic church has traditionally maintained? To us, these and many other similar questions are of such obvious importance that any modern biographer would be bound to answer them. We think that we can only really understand a person when we have recognized the influences on them in their formative years, but the gospel writers, like everyone else in the ancient world, thought differently.

There is nothing wrong with the biography of Jesus which we find in the gospels, once we recognize that the gospel writers were biographers in the ancient, not the modern mould. Biographers in the ancient world could take one of two courses. They could either pass over their subject's childhood in virtual silence, or fill their pages with fantastic tales of his prodigious youthful achievements. The gospel writers provided several stories of prodigies around the birth of Jesus, but (with the exception of a single story in Luke's gospel) said nothing of his childhood. However, in their treatment of the child Jesus they have answered the key question any biographer has to tackle; the question of what sort of a man this person was. But each one did it in his own way.

Stories of Jesus' birth

Take Matthew's gospel first. It strikes us as odd that he should have chosen to begin his gospel with something as dull as a genealogy. Our familiar Christmas readings skip over the first seventeen verses of Matthew, and begin with what interests us, the vivid stories surrounding Jesus' birth. But Matthew's contemporaries would have seen things differently. When the Jewish historian Josephus (c.37–c.100AD) undertook to write his autobiography, he too began with his genealogy

(Josephus, *Life* 3–6 (1)). Although he only traced his ancestry back five generations, it was sufficient to establish his claim to be of priestly descent. Then, as with the gospels, Josephus virtually passed over his early life altogether. For Matthew and his readers, as for Josephus and his, to know who someone was you had to know, not about his upbringing, but about his family.

And Matthew had further reasons for writing as he did. Matthew was concerned that the Christian converts reading his gospel (or more likely hearing it read) should recognize that Jesus was descended from Abraham through David, and that the great turning-points of the history of God's people have occurred at set intervals. Jesus' birth occurred at the close of one such interval, fourteen generations from the Exile. Matthew achieved these aims by means of his schematized genealogy at the very start of the gospel (Matt 1:1–17). Matthew was writing for readers who assumed that the birth of a great man would be attended by omens and portents. For this reason, he drew attention to the divinely-ordained dreams of Joseph, which reassured Joseph that he should take Mary as his wife, spoke of the child's future ministry, and directed the movements of the holy family (Matt 1:20, 21; 2:13, 19, 22). His main story of the birth itself takes a portent as its central theme: the star seen by the magi (Matt 2:1–12). His readers would also expect to be told in what ways Jesus, even in his birth, fulfilled the prophecies of the Old Testament scriptures (Matt 1:22f; 2:4–6, 15, 17–23). The fact that Matthew provided these features does not prove that he simply invented them. Matthew included them because he was inspired to recognize in them the signs to him and to his readers that God's saving purposes were focused in the baby of Bethlehem and the boy of Nazareth. (On the historical basis of these stories, see Witherington 1992 60–74, and Brown 1993[2] 503–562).

Luke had a rather different audience in mind when writing his gospel. At the start of his gospel he named a person to whom he was writing, Theophilus (probably the patron of the book who met the expenses of publishing), and set out the programme for his work: 'to write an orderly narrative for you . . . so as to give you authentic knowledge about the matters of which you have been informed' (Lk.1:1–4).

If Matthew expected his readers to be familiar with Old Testament passages and allusions, and therefore seems to have had in mind an audience at least on the fringes of Judaism, Luke by way of contrast appears to be writing for Gentiles. But Gentile readers, too, expected to hear of portents and prophecies surrounding the birth of a great man. The

Roman writer Quintilian (c.35–c.100AD), whose work as an educator we encountered in the previous chapter, advised that when writing a man's life, any oracles or prophecies which foretold the man's birth should be included in the opening part of the work (*Institutio Oratoriae* 3.7). Luke seems to have been of the same opinion, and devoted a good deal of space to the intertwined events surrounding the births of Jesus and of John, his herald. Luke did not take the prophecies of the Old Testament as his basis, but presented those which sprang up freshly around the child to be born (Lk.1:30–7, 42–45, 46–55, 67–79) as well as the oracles which pointed to the greatness of the newborn baby (2:10–12 28–32, 34f., 38).

The gospel record of the childhood of Jesus

When we move from the birth of Jesus to his childhood, we are confronted again with the differences between the ancient perspective and a modern one. A modern reader is not surprised to read of the birth of Jesus in the gospels, even if it is not presented in the way we would expect. But a modern reader *is* surprised to find that virtually nothing is said of the childhood of Jesus, the period we would think of as a person's formative years. Matthew sees nothing of interest between the holy family's move from Egypt to Nazareth (which is of interest to him because of the double fulfilment of prophecy: Matt.2:15, 23) and the beginning of John's ministry of baptism. Luke has a plain summary of Jesus' growth (Lk.2:40) and one isolated story from Jesus's boyhood (Lk.2:41–52).

Even more surprisingly, Mark and John omit all references to Jesus' birth and childhood. Mark begins his story with John the Baptist's preaching; John with the Word which was in the beginning with God, before going on to relate John's ministry. For Mark and John, it was John the Baptist's ministry, not Jesus' own childhood, which formed the necessary background to help us understand him.

But we should notice that each of the evangelists has explained who and what Jesus is, even though they did not do so in the developmental terms which we would use today.

Matthew had established all he needed to establish for his readers by the story of Jesus' birth. If you read carefully the whole of Matthew 1 and 2, noting all that is said about Jesus, and all that is implied in the repeated instances of fulfilled prophecy, you will have, as Matthew intended you should, a pretty clear idea of who Jesus is: both the Son of

David, divinely begotten and born in fulfilment of prophecy, and also a vulnerable child, already drawing around himself the menace of hostile powers. Stories of his childhood would have been superfluous.

Luke, too, had told his readers who the child is: the Messiah, the Lord: (Lk.2:11). But he emphasized the oracles which suggested what the child would do: before Jesus was born, there were Gabriel's prophecy (Lk.1:30–3), and Mary's song (Lk.1:46–55); at his birth the angels proclaimed him deliverer, Messiah and Lord (Lk.2:10–12); the visit of the holy family to the temple to present the child to the Lord (2:22–24) was the opportunity for two further oracles, those of Simeon (2:28–32, 34f.) and of Anna (Lk.2:38).

Luke also finds space for a single story from Jesus' boyhood, or rather from that pivotal age for a Jewish boy, his thirteenth year, when he would be preparing to take his place as an adult in the religious community at his next birthday (Safrai & Stern 1976 772). It would be easy to dismiss this tale as pious fiction, created in order to persuade those who heard it that Jesus was already marked out for greatness at this early age. But, if it is a creation by the church, it is odd that Mary should emerge in such a poor light from the story, lacking comprehension of who and what Jesus was. It is still more difficult to suppose that Luke invented the story himself, when he is foremost in the New Testament in the respect and attention he accorded to Jesus' mother.

In this story (Lk2:41–52) Luke pointed out the remarkable understanding of Jesus even before his religious coming of age. The boy Jesus, who had not yet even taken the yoke of the Torah upon himself, confounds the wisest teachers of the law (2:46f.). It was a common motif of biography in the ancient world to emphasize the prodigious characteristics in the childhood of a great man. Josephus, with a certain amount of conceit, told a rather similar story about himself at around fourteen years of age, claiming that he was already sought out by the leading men of Jerusalem so that they might hear his opinion on matters of the law (Josephus, *Life*, 9 (2)).

Luke's very restrained story shows that the promise of Jesus' infancy was being fulfilled even in his boyhood. It also goes beyond merely drawing attention to Jesus' precocious understanding. It suggests that Jesus, although belonging to the family at Nazareth, had a Father whose claims upon him were prior to those of his human family (Lk.2:49). Jesus would later have much to say about the potential conflict between the demands of kinship, so strong in the agrarian society of Palestine, and the demands of the kingdom of God. In this story the twelve-year-old

Jesus was already beginning to show that there could be tension between conforming to what society expected and 'being about his father's business'. In this story, too, the prophecies about him begin to be fulfilled; as Mary's heart is troubled (2:48f.), as Simeon had foretold (2:35).

The significance of the childhood stories of Jesus

What, then, is the significance of the way in which the gospels treat Jesus the child?

First, the almost total silence about Jesus' childhood is very noticeable. Christian devotion and curiosity eventually demanded more stories about Jesus as a child, especially more early portents and childhood prodigies, than the canonical gospels provided. So there arose from the second century onwards the so-called 'Infancy Gospels', notably the Gospels of Thomas and of James, which provided more stories about the boy Jesus.

We should not expect these late compositions to tell us anything authentic about the child Jesus. In the Gospel of Thomas, for instance, we find some stories which are simply bizarre, like that of Jesus helping Joseph in his carpentry work by pulling a beam of wood so that it stretched to fit the job on which Joseph was engaged. Other stories show a darker aspect, such as the story of a boy who accidentally knocked against the young Jesus when running past. Jesus, in this story, cursed the child so that he fell down and died. Indeed, everyone who crossed or annoyed the child Jesus was likely to meet the same end. The fact that later in the story he restored all those whom he had cursed does not remove the impression that in these Infancy Gospels, Jesus has become little more than a powerful sorcerer. This, no doubt, is how some early Christians understood him, and the writers of the Infancy Gospels invented their narratives partly to entertain their readers and partly to portray the kind of Jesus they believed in. Their concern to speak to their readers had totally eclipsed their concern with the historical realities of Jesus' life.

The excesses of these Infancy Gospels remind us, by way of contrast, of the restraint with which the canonical gospel writers proceeded. Stories of prodigious deeds in the infancy of a hero were the stock-in-trade of ancient biography. The canonical gospels have no such stories, apart from Luke's single story of Jesus at twelve years old. Their very restraint gives us reason to believe that the circumstances of Jesus' life were not eclipsed in their picture by their concern for the present relevance of the story they had to tell.

Second, the very fact that Matthew and Luke chose to include the birth of Jesus in their gospel narratives had momentous consequences.

Their infancy stories had consequences for the Christian understanding of Christ. Some early Christians had difficulty in believing that the person Jesus had always been the Christ and the Son of God. Some thought that he only became Son of God at some point in his adult life, perhaps at his baptism when the Holy Spirit descended upon him. This was the view known as 'Adoptionism': the baby and child Jesus were merely the human being into whom the divine nature was going to enter. Mark's gospel, for instance, with its silence about Jesus' life before his baptism, would not be able to counter this. But Matthew and Luke showed clearly, by including their infancy stories, that all that Jesus was, he was from the outset of his life. They left little room to believe that Jesus the child was different in nature from Jesus the man.

The inclusion of the birth narratives also had consequences for the Christian understanding of childhood. Not everyone found it easy to believe that the baby in the Bethlehem manger was fully God as well as fully human. 'I deny', wrote Nestorius in the early fifth century, 'that God is two months or three months old' (in Cyril of Alexandria, *Epistle* 23). Nestorius, and others, were not crude Adoptionists, but they wanted to believe that the divine nature in Christ was so separate from his human nature that it was spared the experience of infancy. The church as a whole condemned Nestorius; it was one person, fully God and fully human, who lay in the manger, and who grew up at Nazareth. The birth narratives were not the only reason why the church came to this conclusion, but they played a part in persuading the church that in Christ, God had himself entered fully into human experience. And if the incarnate Christ had assumed the experiences of childhood, as well as those of adult life, then childhood itself took on a new dignity and importance.

Jesus and Children

In order to appreciate Jesus' sayings and actions concerning children, we have to realize that they were not just isolated incidents. They fitted into the overall pattern of his ministry, which was organized around the central theme of the arrival of the kingdom of God. So we need, first, to grasp what Jesus meant by 'the kingdom of God', and then where children fitted into it.

Children and the kingdom of God

When we speak of a 'kingdom', we generally mean a territory, such as the United Kingdom, ruled over by a monarch. For Jesus and his contemporaries, 'kingdom' meant the activity of being a king, something more like 'rule' or 'reign'. So the 'kingdom of God' meant 'God ruling as king'.

Of course Jewish people of Jesus' day believed that God already ruled the world which he had made. The Scriptures told them as much (Is.6:5; Ps.29:10; 99:1–4). But by the time of Jesus they had also come to believe that there would be a final intervention of God in history, when he would bring his purpose of redemption to fulfilment (see Dan 7). God's reign, or kingdom, would break into this world in such a way that the present order of sin and of suffering would be done away with, sin punished, and God's people vindicated. The striking thing about Jesus' ministry was his proclamation that the kingdom of God was already present among people during his ministry. God had already taken the decisive step of establishing his rule, in and through Jesus himself.

To be sure, God's reign was also still to come in its fulness. There was a day, still to come, when the kingdom of God would bring the course of this world to a close (Mk.13:24–37). But in the ministry of Jesus, the kingdom of God was already present and active. Jesus' healings and exorcisms displayed the presence of the kingdom (Matt.12:28). Many of Jesus' parables invite his hearers to picture how the kingdom, which is already here, can be working in the world and be recognized by some, but overlooked by many (Mk.4:26–32; Matt.13:33).

The kingdom of God was something to be entered. When Jesus spoke about the kingdom, he invited people to enter it. Jesus' contemporaries might have expected that if there was such a kingdom, then the first to enter it would be the pious and revered teachers of the Law, the scribes and Pharisees. But the kingdom of God, Jesus said, turned human expectations upside down. The kingdom of God was a realm of surprises. In one of his enigmatic sayings, Jesus commented that: 'Many who are first will be last, and the last first' (Matt.19:30, Mk.10:31, Lk.13:30, cf. Matt.20:16). He was referring, perhaps, to the surprises which the day of judgement would bring (Matt.25:31–46). But it was a saying with relevance to the present too. The most forward in entering the kingdom of God proved to be, not the scribes and other respected people, but the most despised members of society: 'Truly I tell you: tax-collectors and prostitutes are entering the kingdom of God ahead of you (chief priests and elders)' (Matt.21:31).

Jesus' ministry embraced many of the most marginal people in the society of his day, and the coming of the kingdom of God was good news (gospel) for them. Some people, like tax-collectors or prostitutes, were regarded as outcasts because of their occupations. Others, like lepers or the demon-possessed, were pushed to the edge of the community because of their afflictions (Mk.1:40–5, 5:1–20). To people like these, Jesus offered the new life of the kingdom of God. Forgiveness, healing and deliverance, were blessings to be received in the kingdom of God.

Where, then, did children fit into the pattern of God's kingship? They were, after all, also marginal people, as has been seen in the previous chapter. What did the kingdom of God mean for children, and what did Jesus have to say about them?

Children were models for discipleship in the kingdom of God. In Jesus' view, they both pointed the way for adults to enter the kingdom of God, and showed how adults were to follow Jesus in the kingdom of God.

Entering the kingdom: Mark 10:13–16

Jesus called on those who heard him to enter the kingdom of God. But how was this to be done? What sort of people could enter? In one of his enigmatic sayings, Jesus took children as the model for this key issue of entry into the kingdom of God:

> They brought children for him to touch. The disciples rebuked them, but when Jesus saw it, he was indignant, and said to them, 'Let the children come to me; do not try to stop them; for the kingdom of God belongs to such as these. Truly I tell you: whoever does not accept the kingdom of God like a child will never enter it.' And he put his arms around them, laid his hands on them, and blessed them. (Mk.10:13–16. See also Matt.19:13–15; 18:3, Lk.18:15–17)

One of the most characteristic features of Jesus' teaching was his ability to intrigue people and give them puzzling sayings in which they had to find the meaning for themselves. This is such a saying. What does it imply about the kingdom of God and about children? It highlights that entry into the kingdom is not by way of merit, privilege and status. The kingdom of God turns the values of the world upside-down. In the world it is the worthy who are the first in society, but in the kingdom of God, the unworthy enter first (Matt.21:31). Normally it is the adult who supplies the model for the child to imitate. But in the kingdom of God, the adult is to follow the child. Significantly, Mark has put this story and the next one we shall consider (Mk.9:33–7), in the central block of his gospel (Mk.8:27–10:45), which contains Jesus' teachings, by word and example, about the meaning of discipleship.

In the previous chapter we looked at the emphasis placed in Jewish society on socialisation of children, especially the instruction of boys in the Torah. The Jewish community put a high value on producing new generations which would walk in the ways of their ancestors, children moulded into the ways of the adults. But in entering the kingdom of God it is the other way round: it is children who supply the model for adults. Adults have something of crucial importance to learn from children.

The story itself shows how open Jesus was to children. Mark does not tell us precisely who brought the children to Jesus. Presumably it was the parents who wished their children (Luke says: 'even babies', Lk.18:15 - author's translation) to receive a blessing from this holy teacher. The disciples tried to prevent them, in all probability because they did not think that children were worthy of the Master's attention. We shall return a little later to the role of parents and disciples in this story. But, turning our attention to Jesus, we see that he wanted the children to have as full access to him as adults might have. He received them quite literally with open arms and gave them the blessing for which the parents had asked, and which the disciples would have denied them.

As in other incidents in the gospels, we notice the importance of touch in Jesus' ministry. Here Jesus took children in his arms, a physical gesture which symbolized his protection and care. Mark alone mentions that 'he put his arms round them' (Mk.10:16). Matthew mentions only the laying-on of hands, for blessing, and Luke omits all reference to Jesus' gestures. Quite often Matthew and Luke leave out picturesque details which are present in Mark's narrative, and perhaps in this instance they felt the 'cuddle' was unnecessary to the story, or even undignified. Some later scribes changed 'he put his arms around them' to 'he called them to himself' (only a slight change in the Greek), so it seems likely that some early Christians did find the idea of Jesus 'cuddling' the children rather lacking in appropriate dignity. It is probable that Mark's picture preserves the remembrance of Jesus' contact with the children; his actions as well as his words.

Was there something unusual or even unique about Jesus' approach to children? It appears that there was, but it was not that he uniquely thought children were important while his contemporaries did not. Our investigation of Jewish education in the previous chapter showed us that the Jewish community was not neglectful of children. Quite the reverse: children were highly regarded as a blessing from God. They were protected by Jewish law and custom from the dangers to which Gentile children were open, such as exposure at birth. The rabbis made provision for teaching children, and for their thorough initiation into the ways of their ancestors. But Jesus' openness to children was for their own sake, not principally for their potential, and it was something unique to his ministry.

To turn from Jesus' actions in this story to his words: what did Jesus mean by saying that 'the kingdom of God belongs to such as these'? We might think that he was idealizing children, imputing to them particular qualities such as innocence, which made them morally superior to adults, or unclouded spiritual perception, which made them more responsive to unseen realities. Wordsworth eloquently drew out such an understanding of childhood in his *Ode on Intimations of Immortality from Recollections of Early Childhood*:

> Not in entire forgetfulness,
> And not in utter nakedness,
> But trailing clouds of glory do we come
> From God who is our home:
> Heaven lies about us in our infancy!

Some remarks of Jesus in the gospels do certainly suggest that Jesus regarded children as more open to revelation of the truth than adults might be (see the comments below on Matt.11:25; 18:10).

But Jesus was, to judge from his sayings as well as his deeds, a realist about human nature; he was equally realistic about the nature of children, to judge from his observations on a children's game.

How can I describe this generation? They are like children sitting in the market-place and calling to each other, 'We piped for you and you would not dance. We lamented, and you would not mourn'. For John [the Baptist] came, neither eating nor drinking, and people say, 'He is possessed'; the Son of Man came, eating and drinking, and they say, 'Look at him! A glutton and a drinker, a friend of tax-collectors and sinners!' Yet God's wisdom is proved right by its results. (Matt.11:16–19, cf. Lk.7:31–35)

We do not know what the point of this little game was. Was it a stylized game, in which one side were the performers, and the other the audience, and in which the inappropriate responses were all part of the game? Or had Jesus noticed a game gone wrong, and this complaint of the children was a spontaneous reaction to friends who were not sticking to the rules? Either interpretation is possible. But the important point is that he knew how children, in their play, act out roles in which they exercise power over others. In this context, he could recognize the same pattern of childhood role-play in the adult reactions to him and to John. There was, in any case, no sentimentality in Jesus' view of children.

Jesus was speaking specifically about how a person enters the kingdom of God, and in looking at children it was not their subjective characteristics, but their objective position in society which made them models for discipleship. He meant that just as children occupied a socially inferior position, dependent on others, and at the beck and call of others, so also his followers must live as servants in the kingdom. To enter the kingdom of God means to renounce self and self-seeking and to take a status of no consequence. In Jesus' own language, Aramaic, as well as in Greek (the language in which the gospels were written) 'child' and 'servant' are the same words. The life of the kingdom of God is a life of service and humility, exemplified by the place taken by children, the people of least consequence in the power structure of the family and of the wider society.

So, in saying 'the kingdom of God belongs to such as these', Jesus was saying something about the sort of person who enters the kingdom. But was he also saying something about children themselves? Did he mean 'the kingdom of God belongs to people who take a place of humility equivalent to that of children (but it does not belong to children themselves)'? Some commentators have understood his words in this way. But surely, we must let his action interpret his words in this incident. Jesus received the children to himself. By his action he suggested that his words mean 'the kingdom of God belongs to children such as these (let them be your model)'. He was making a statement in word and action about children and their importance in the kingdom of God. But his words had implications for those adults who would be his disciples.

And what of the second part of Jesus' saying, the comment that 'whoever does not accept the kingdom of God like a child will never enter it'? Some commentators have suggested that the meaning is 'whoever does not accept the kingdom of God as they would accept a child, will never enter it'. This is a possible meaning, but not as probable as the alternative, that the kingdom of God has to be received in a childlike way. This leads to a further question: what particular quality of childlikeness is in view here? Elsewhere in his teaching, Jesus condemned double-mindedness, and the inability to concentrate on the one thing necessary in following him. Perhaps in this instance, the quality Jesus commends from the example of children is the opposite of that – the childlike ability to give oneself wholly to some pursuit, without holding back. Matthew does not have this saying, but gives a similar one in Matt.18:3 (see below, pp.57f).

The gospel writers provide a commentary on the meaning of this incident by the context into which they put it in their narratives. In each of the three gospels in which it is found, this story is followed immediately by the story of the rich man who was confident that he had kept the commandments, but who could not follow Jesus because he had too much to lose (Matt.19:16–30, Mk.10:17–31, Lk.18:18–30). The man provides a contrast to the children who are not encumbered by property, possessions and power. So the two scenes – the children who receive Jesus' blessing and the rich man who cannot follow Jesus – serve to highlight and contrast each other.

Matthew and Mark also preface this story with Jesus' saying about marriage and divorce (Matt.19:1–12, Mk.10:1–12). This may suggest that they were trying to bring together a short compendium on Jesus' teaching on the household (marriage – children – possessions). Such a grouping of Jesus' teaching would be a reminder that the first Christians did not give children an independent place within the church, but that children were regarded principally as part of the households which made up the Christian communities. Matthew and Mark put the topic of 'children' under the heading of 'home and family'. This appears to have been the common approach of the early church, and we shall return to this point in the next chapter. Luke, on the other hand, prefaces the story with the parable of the Pharisee and the tax-collector (Lk.18:9–14), which is aimed, as Luke puts it, 'at those who were sure of their own goodness, and looked down on everyone else'. In this way he draws attention to the fact that children, like the tax-collector and unlike the Pharisee, have no goodness or virtue to parade in front of others.

Since at least the end of the second century, this passage, especially the words, 'Let the children come to me, do not try to stop them', have been taken as a justification of infant baptism (see below, p.86). In the context of Jesus' ministry it is unlikely that they had this reference. But as Mark and the other gospel-writers recorded them, they may already have had the practice of infant baptism in mind, and may have taken

Jesus' words as a justification of it. Our decision as to whether the gospel writers could or could not have taken Jesus' words in this way will depend, of course, on the view we take of the origins of infant baptism; whether it was there at the beginnings of the Christian church, or arose much later on. This topic will be the subject of our attention in chapter four.

Life in the kingdom: Mark 9:33–7, 42

There is a second saying in which Jesus spoke of the significance of children in the kingdom of God:

> So they came to Capernaum; and when he had gone indoors, he asked them, 'What were you arguing about on the way?' They were silent, because on the way they had been discussing which of them was the greatest. So he sat down, called the Twelve, and said to them, 'If anyone wants to be first, he must make himself last of all and servant of all'. Then he took a child, set him in front of them, and put his arm round him. 'Whoever receives a child like this in my name,' he said, 'receives me; and whoever receives me, receives not me but the One who sent me'.

> 'If anyone causes the downfall of one of these little ones who believe, it would be better for him to be thrown into the sea with a millstone round his neck'. (Mark 9:33–7, 42, cf. Matt.18:1-7, Lk.9:46–8, 17:1–2).

Here the issue is greatness among Jesus' disciples. Mark presents this as a straighforward squabble over precedence, but Matthew gives it a more spiritual tone by adding 'in the kingdom of heaven': 'Who is the greatest in the kingdom of heaven?' (Matt 18:1). A keen interest in status now (Mark) and status in the coming kingdom (Matthew) is understandable, not only in the general human (perhaps characteristically male) concern with prestige, but also, and more particularly, in the context of the religious life of Palestine in the early first century. The religious community whose written records have been found at Qumran by the Dead Sea, and which was flourishing in the time of Jesus, was very interested in matters of ranking and status among its members. It was highly structured and hierarchical; as one of its documents says, 'No man shall raise himself above the place to which his lot assigns him' (1QS2.23). The Community Rule suggests that they saw their current hierarchy as an anticipation of the hierarchy of the coming kingdom. So the disciples' question about status reveals that they were assuming that there would be a similar hierarchical ranking within the community forming around Jesus, now and in the coming kingdom.

Jesus' reply clearly dismisses this kind of speculation, and sets out a vision of an entirely different kind of greatness. But Mark and Matthew draw out complementary meanings from the saying. Mark concentrates attention on how greatness is seen in the treatment of the least significant person, of whom the child is a ready example; Matthew on how children are an example to disciples. So it is worth examining each account separately.

In Mark, this saying is put in the context of Jesus' teaching on the meaning of discipleship. Jesus took the child to himself after saying that to be first in the kingdom of God, one must become last. Then, with his arm around the child, he went on to speak about receiving a child like that in his name. The theme is still greatness in the kingdom, but Mark's presentation of the saying emphasizes that true greatness consists in receiving those who are unimportant in the eyes of the world, and receiving them in the name of Christ. 'Receiving' here probably means serving someone and seeing to their needs, and the child is taken as a ready example of the weak and powerless. Jesus expanded the significance of what he had said with the claim that to receive a child like that in his name is to receive him, and to receive him is to receive the One who sent him.

We may well have to understand this saying in the light of the Jewish law of agency. A later rabbinical saying held that: 'A man's agent is like himself' (*Ber.* 5.5). Such authorized representatives or proxies were to be received and treated like the person whom they represented. This seems to have been a long-established and widely-recognized aspect of Jewish society. It had developed from the ancient Semitic customs surrounding messengers, who had to be given plenipotentiary powers to act on their masters' behalf, because of the difficulties of communicating over long distances. An example would be Abraham's servant, dealing on his master's behalf with the betrothal of Isaac (Gen. 24). Respect shown to such agents was shown to the one whom they represented. In saying 'Whoever receives a child like this in my name receives me; and whoever receives me, receives not me but the One who sent me', Jesus was drawing on the imagery of this custom or law of agency.

The saying which we are considering here has clear implications, when seen in this light, for the person of Jesus himself, as the agent or representative of the One who sent him. But it also underlines the significance which he accorded to children. In their treatment of children, the disciples turn out to be dealing, not (as they might think) with the least important members of society, but with their master's chosen representatives. Jesus is not here drawing attention to a proxy's power to act on his master's behalf. Rather, he is pointing to the duty of honour, respect and care which is to be shown to a master through the treatment of those whom he has chosen to represent his name. When they received one such child in Christ's name, the disciples were receiving him; they should treat the child with respect and care, as if they were receiving Christ himself. Just as they would receive a man's authorized representative with the same honour they would bestow on the man himself, so they should regard and receive a child as Christ's authorized representative. We find a similar emphasis on the profound importance of service to the weak in the parable of the Sheep and Goats (Matt.25:31–46): at the Last Day it will be seen that service given to the weak and needy has been given to Jesus himself.

This passage from Mark 9, in which Jesus begins by speaking about 'a child like this', and ends by speaking of 'these little ones who believe', raises one of the most acute questions to do with children in the gospels: how far, and in what places, was Jesus speaking literally of children, and to what extent was he using the figure of a 'child' to refer to other groups of people, whether the poor in society, or the weak and insignificant among his own followers? We must give some attention to this important question raised by our passage.

Some scholars find it unlikely that Jesus should have spoken in this way about children. Particularly in his sayings about 'receiving' children, or causing 'little ones' to stumble, he must have been speaking metaphorically, using the image of a child to speak about adult disciples. Scholars have noted that disciples were addressed as 'children' in the early church (1 Jn.4:4; 5:21). They have drawn attention also to the fact that, in Matthew 10:42, the expression 'little ones' is used in a way which seems to refer specifically to adults: 'Truly I tell you: anyone who gives so much as a cup of cold water to one of these little ones because he is a disciple of mine, will certainly not go unrewarded'. In that passage, Jesus was giving mission instructions, so that 'receiving' in that context must mean 'taking an itinerant disciple into one's home'. It is unlikely that these 'little ones' can, therefore, be children. From these observations, scholars have drawn the conclusion that the main focus of interest in the sayings about 'little ones', and probably about children, too, lies in the disciples, or in the poor who respond to Jesus' ministry, and not in physical children at all.

So, in Mark 9 and Matthew 18, it is commonly supposed by commentators that the specific person of the child with which the discourse began, recedes rapidly into the background, and that the 'little ones who believe' are adult disciples.

The conviction of scholars that when the gospels speak of 'children' they really mean 'adults' has its effect in the interpretation of other passages: in Matthew 11:25 and Luke 10:21, the New English Bible and Revised English Bible translators have chosen to render the Greek word *nepioi*, literally 'little children', as 'the simple', giving the translation: 'I thank you Father, Lord of heaven and earth, for hiding these things from the learned and wise, and revealing them to the simple'. The translators are aiming to express what most commentators believe to have been the meaning of Jesus' words: that although important truths ('these things') have been hidden from the wise and learned, they have been revealed to those who have no wisdom or learning. A contrast is probably intended with the teachers of the Law, who enjoyed such prestige in the society of Judaea and Galilee.

But, as with Jesus' words 'the kingdom of God belongs to such as these', we should allow the possibility that in each of these sayings he was indeed speaking, in the first instance, about children themselves. For one thing, we should let the narrative interpret the sayings. So, with the saying about revealing truths to 'little ones', we find that when Jesus entered the temple and had driven out the traders and money-changers, it was the children who acclaimed him with the shout 'Hosanna to the Son of David', while the chief priests and scribes were indignant (Matt.21:15). Matthew relates an incident in which the truth was hidden from the learned and wise, but revealed to the children, precisely the issue raised by Matthew 11:25.

If children appeared in Jesus' sayings and in the stories about him, only as illustrations of weakness, frailty or lack of power, then there would be a strong case for thinking that the main interest he had in children was as a parabolic means of highlighting aspects of adult disciples' lives. But in fact, children found their way into several of Jesus' sayings, and not merely those in which a child was the centre of attention. He noticed the atmosphere of children's play, as was noted in the comments on Matthew 11:16–19 (p.50f). In Luke 11:7 the crowded intimacy of a poor family is brought before us in the words of the householder who will not go to the door in the night: 'The door is already closed, and my children are with me in the bed' (author's translation). Concerning prayer we have the saying: 'Would any of you offer his son a stone when he asks for bread, or a snake when he asks for a fish? If you, bad as you are, know how to give good things to your children, how much more will your heavenly Father give good things to those who ask him!' (Matt.7:9–11, parallel, with differences, to Lk.11:11–13).

The family relationship of child and parent was central to Jesus' presentation of the life of discipleship. It is no coincidence that Jesus' own prayers were phrased in family terms. He spoke to God as *Abba*, and taught his followers to do the same. This was a word without the childishness of the English 'Daddy', but quite clearly charged with the intimacy of family life (Barr 1988). Disciples using that address in prayer put themselves as children before God.

Children interested Jesus. References to children, encounters with children and imagery drawn from the world of children are woven into the fabric of Jesus' ministry in a remarkable way. The terms 'little ones' and 'little children' may well have an extended reference to adult disciples, but Jesus did not lose sight of real children. The way that Jesus' sayings about children have been presented in the gospels certainly gives the impression that the evangelists, as they passed on Jesus' words, were mainly interested in the implications of Jesus' sayings for the direction of adult lives. But Jesus himself gave particular significance to children.

So we may suppose that where there is some reason for connecting 'little ones' with real children, we are justified in doing so. Mark 9 is such a passage. After speaking of receiving the child, Mark goes on to give the story about the exorcist who was not a disciple, but who still used the name of Jesus (Mk.9:38–41). He develops the theme of using the name of Jesus and of receiving people in his name. But in verse 42, Mark returns to the topic of children and notes Jesus' saying about causing one of 'these little ones who believe to fall', by which he means stumbling or faltering in faith and discipleship. Jesus stresses that to cause this is a grave matter, and continues with a series of warnings about a disciple's own liability to fall (Mk.9:43–50). Again, we see that Jesus took children with total seriousness, and that what happens to a child, and to a child's faith, is a matter of great consequence to those who are in the kingdom of God.

Luke emphasized Jesus' identification with the child by saying that Jesus put the child 'by his side' (Lk.9:47). Luke also made explicit that Jesus was speaking of a particular child: 'Whoever receives *this child* in my name receives me' (Lk.9:48).

Matthew organized his material differently. In Matthew's version of the story, Jesus put the child in front of the disciples before speaking. The child whom Jesus set before the disciples thus serves as a sort of visual aid:

'Truly I tell you: unless you turn round and become like children, you will never enter the kingdom of heaven. Whoever humbles himself and becomes like this child will be the greatest in the kingdom of heaven' (Matt.18:3–4).

Matthew has put this saying at the head of a section on discipline within the Christian community (Matt.18). In this context, the child provides a vital model to all disciples, and in particular to those called to leadership. Discipleship involves voluntarily taking on the servant-like, social role of the child. To do that requires nothing less than a reversal of the normal values of our lives. The child helps the disciples see the paradox of life in the kingdom; that to become the greatest in the kingdom, you have to become the least. So, too, they can see the foolishness of their initial question about who is the greatest in the kingdom. The paradox is spelt out in Jesus' words in Mark, 'If anyone wants to be first, he must make himself last of all and servant of all' (Mk.9:35), or more starkly in Luke, 'The least among you all is the greatest' (Lk.9:48). As Matthew appears to be setting out Jesus' teaching on community, the contrast with Qumran is noticeable (see above, p.53). A disciple of his is not to think in terms of status and hierarchy, but to turn and become as a child.

Matthew does not use the story of the exorcist – it does not fit his purpose of teaching on discipline. So he continues from 'receiving a child' in Jesus' name (Matt.18:5) to 'causing a little one who believes to stumble', with the consequent teaching about causes of stumbling (Matt.18:6–9). After this Matthew has a saying preserved only in his gospel: 'See that you do not despise one of these little ones; I tell you, they have their angels in heaven, who look continually on the face of my heavenly Father' (Matt.18:10). Belief in angels was commonplace in the Jewish society of Jesus' day. The specific belief referred to here seems to be the notion that each person has an angel corresponding to them, who also resembles them (see Acts 12:15). Jesus' words in Matthew 18:10 mean, therefore, that the angels of children are of the very highest order – they look directly upon God. The worth and diginity of children may be seen from the exalted rank of the angels which represent them. They are not to be despised, or counted as of little worth. The truth about children is indeed quite the opposite: in God's sight their worth cannot be exaggerated.

Children and the Disciples

Children provided an example for discipleship in the kingdom of God. Unencumbered by either possessions or prejudice, they could see what was hidden from the wise (Matt.11:25; 21:15); set low in social status, they gave an example of life in the kingdom of God (Matt.18:1–4); weak and vulnerable as they were, they were above all to be the focus of the disciples' concern (Mk.9:36f., 42, Matt.18:10).

The disciples did not share Jesus' understanding of children. They attempted to prevent children being brought to Jesus, and rebuked those who brought them (Mk.10:13). In this the disciples reflected the outlook of their surrounding culture; a low estimate of the social standing of children. Part of what they learnt from Jesus was to have his attitude to children.

When we have noted the remarkably positive things which Jesus has to say about children in the kingdom of God, it is a surprise to find a much tougher saying on the subject of children and discipleship. Immediately after the saying about accepting the kingdom of God like a child, there is, as we have seen, the story of the rich man, so weighed down by his wealth that he could not follow Jesus (Mk.10:17–22, Matt.19:16–22, Lk.18:19–23). The man's departure leads into a conversation about wealth and discipleship. Peter summarizes how the disciples experienced what Jesus has said:

> 'What about us?' said Peter. 'We have left everything to follow you.'
> Jesus said, 'Truly I tell you: there is no one who has given up home,
> brothers or sisters, mother, father or children, or land, for my sake and for
> the gospel, who will not receive in this age a hundred times as much -
> houses, brothers and sisters, mothers and children, and land – and
> persecutions besides; and in the age to come eternal life.' (Mk.10:28–30,
> cf. Matt.19:27–9, Lk.18:28–30).

Here, children feature among those relations and responsibilities which may be 'given up' for the sake of Jesus and the gospel, and, more mysteriously, will be received back a hundredfold in this life. Matthew and Luke present the saying rather differently, but 'children' appear in the list of renunciations of all three gospel writers.

This is no callous repudiation of what the gospel writers have just related on the topic of children. Some have indeed supposed that Jesus was inimical to the family, but that conclusion can only be reached by taking a few striking sayings, such as this one, and considering them in isolation. If we look at the whole of Jesus' ministry, his actions as well as his words, the chosen images of his parables and his affirmation of filial and marital responsibilities, then we see a different picture. In the light of the gospels' whole presentation we must recognize that Jesus was not attempting to destroy the family, or to eject children from the family framework in which their lives are set (see Ellis 1985).

What, then, are we to make of this saying? If we read it in the wider context of Jesus' ministry, we are driven to conclude that it cannot have been meant to encourage the estrangement of children and parents, which is indeed identified by Jesus as one of the dreadful marks of the distress of the last days (Mk.13:12). By contrast, in Luke's birth narrative the angel tells John the Baptist's father, Zechariah, that John will fulfil the prophecy of Malachi by reconciling father and child (Lk.1:17), while in Mark 7:9–13 Jesus rebukes the Pharisees for allowing adult children to evade their filial duty of caring for their parents. Rather, what is envisaged here in Mark 10:28–30, is to stress the overriding imperative of following Jesus.

To whom does this imperative apply? It may be that this is not a demand for all disciples, but a reassurance for those who, like Peter, have literally left home and possessions for the sake of following Jesus' itinerant ministry (Peter had long before left his livelihood: Mk.1:18). However, since the subject changes from 'us' to 'whoever', probably all followers of Jesus are in view (Barton 1994 105–7). Perhaps the call here is to leave the secure network of resources and relationships on which the potential disciple depends, rather than to abandon those who depend on him for security and well-being. We would think of children principally as dependants (as they were in Jesus' day too: Matt.7:9–11), but children were also the future providers (see above, p.5), and might even be the parents' present providers (see Mk.7:9–13). All renunciation of the resources of this age for the sake of following Jesus will be rewarded, even in this life (Matthew's version is less specific about this-worldly rewards, but more graphic about the place of the Twelve in the world to come).

Luke has a similar saying in a more radical form: 'If anyone comes to me and does not hate his father and mother, wife and children, brothers and sisters, even his own life, he cannot be a disciple of mine' (Lk.14:26). The 'hate' referred to here is meant to express a strong preference: if you love one thing, you will hate another. No doubt Matthew has correctly discerned this meaning in the saying which he renders as: 'No one is worthy of me who cares more for father or mother than for me; no one is worthy of me who cares more for son or daughter' (Matt.10:37).

The radical thrust of these sayings can probably best be appreciated by taking them in comparison with Mark 3:31–5:

> Then his mother and his brothers arrived; they stayed outside and sent in a message asking him to come out to them. A crowd was sitting round him when word was brought that his mother and brothers were outside asking for him. 'Who are my mother and my brothers?' he replied. And looking round at those who were sitting in the circle about him he said, 'Here are my mother and my brothers. Whoever does the will of God is my brother and sister and mother.' (Mk.3:31–5, cf. Matt.12:46–50, Lk.8:19–21)

Jesus is creating a new community, not merely a collection of individuals. As Jesus himself, so those who follow him will find in that community a new and larger family than the household they had left behind. Even the houses in which they live would be many (if perhaps temporary – see Mk.6:10), and the food they would eat would come from many fields (see Lk.10:7f.). Children are part of that new community.

Here we touch one important but difficult strand of Jesus' ministry: his relativizing of the place of the family. In the Jewish setting, which was the background of his work, the claims of family and kinship were of supreme importance. Individuals were embedded in a network of relationships which mapped out their place in life. People did not float freely through life, but took their place within the grid of kinship into which they had been born. Jesus threw down a challenge to those who lived in this society. He was not proclaiming a rampant individualism, but the creation of a new grouping of even greater importance than the family with its manifold obligations and rewards which would normally dominate a person's life. His own ministry pioneered the way: he, after all, broke with the almost universal convention of Jewish society in his day by not marrying and having children of his own. Such renunciation was not unheard-of in Jewish society, but certainly radical (Barton 1994 23–56).

Here was a challenge to his followers. How far would they be able to bring into reality this vision of a new community? How far would they retain kinship group and household as the building blocks of their lives; and in what ways would they make use of these social units? The answers to those questions come in the story of the early church, to which we shall return in the next chapter.

Children and Parents

On several occasions, already in this chapter, we have allowed the narrative of the gospels to interpret Jesus' sayings. We have to do this again as we consider the practical importance of Jesus' relativizing of the family. Because, although Jesus welcomed children, commended them as examples and spoke of them as objects of care, we find in the gospels that he never actually spoke *to* them. Apart from two words of healing addressed to Jairus's daughter (Mk.5:41), none of the gospel writers record any saying of Jesus spoken to a child, nor any teaching directed at children as a group. Jesus' usual way of relating to children was through their parents.

The parents, we presume, were the people who brought the children for Jesus to bless (Mk.10:13: 'They' brought children for him to touch). And on each occasion when Jesus had to do with specific, individual children, Jesus spoke to the parents. Despite his relativizing of the claims of kinship and family, Jesus did not isolate children from their family settings.

Children appear in the gospel narratives mainly as a focus of parental concern. As we saw in the previous chapter, this is not surprising in view of the high rate of infant mortality and illness widespread in first-century communities. A holy teacher with the reputation of a powerful healer and exorcist would be widely sought after.

The first such appearance of a needy child in Mark's gospel, is in the story of Jairus's daughter. Jairus, a synagogue president, pleaded with Jesus to heal his young daughter (Mk.5:21–4, 35–43, Matt.9:18f., 23–6, Lk.8:40–2, 49–56). By the time Jesus arrived at the house, the mourners were convinced that the child had died, though, as the gospel writers tell the story, it is equally possible that the reader is meant to take Jesus' words literally: 'The child is not dead, she is asleep'. Jesus summoned the father of the child to faith, and went into the room where she was, accompanied by her parents and by his inner group of disciples, Peter, James and John. The raising (or healing) of the child was performed simply: Jesus took her by the hand and spoke to her. Mark records the Aramaic words he used, '*Talitha cum*', and then, in case his readers should think this was some sort of magic incantation, immediately translates them: 'Get up, little girl'. The girl got up and was restored to her parents.

A little later in Mark's gospel, a young daughter features again in a parental request, but this time it was a mother who asked for Jesus' help;

it was a Gentile who made the request, and the girl was afflicted by 'an unclean spirit' (Mk.7:24–30, Matt.15:21–8). In contrast to the incident with Jairus, Jesus showed reluctance rather than willingness, to help. The 'children' whom Jesus is to 'feed' were the people of Israel: 'Let the children be satisfied first; it is not right to take the children's bread and throw it to the dogs', as Jesus graphically put it (Mk.7:27). But the distressed mother had a ready reply: 'Sir, even the dogs under the table eat the children's scraps' (Mk.7:28). For this word of faith, Jesus granted her request, and the girl was freed of her affliction.

The third incident involving the healing of a child in Mark's gospel, is that of the boy whose father approached Jesus' disciples to deliver him from an unclean spirit (Mk.9:14–29, Matt.17:14–21, Lk.9:37–43). Again Jesus elicited a declaration of faith from the parent (Mk.9:24) and then delivered the boy from his trouble (Mk.9:25–7). And, as with Jairus's daughter, people supposed that the child was dead, but Jesus raised him, taking him by the hand.

In Matthew 8:5–13, Luke 7:1–10 and John 4:46–54 we have the story of the healing of one of the household of an officer at Capernaum (if indeed, John's narrative is a different form of the same episode, and not, as some scholars conclude, a different story altogether). In Luke's version, the sick person is a 'slave'; in John's version, he is the man's 'son'; Matthew describes him ambiguously as a *pais*, which could mean either a servant or a child. John certainly, and Matthew possibly, saw this as the healing of a child. Again, as with the incidents in Mark, it is the adult, the household head, who speaks for the child and exercises faith on his behalf.

Finally in our catalogue of incidents involving children in the gospels, there is the raising of the widow of Nain's son. It is a story unique to Luke's gospel and it follows directly on from the 'slave' at Capernaum (Lk.7:11–17). Clearly there is no question of the son exercising faith in this incident, but it is significant that Jesus' compassion is directed towards the widow (Lk.7:13) rather than towards the boy.

From these incidents of healing and exorcism, we see that in the gospel writers' presentation, children are spoken for, rather than speaking for themselves, in their encounters with Jesus. In the usual form of an adult's encounter with Jesus for exorcism or healing, the one seeking healing speaks to Jesus (though not invariably, see Mk.2:1–5). Yet, in all the encounters of Jesus with children, the approach is from the parents on behalf of the children, and Jesus' response is to the parents for the children. On a number of occasions in the gospels Jesus asked adults to demonstrate their faith, commended them for their faith, or criticized them for its absence. On no occasion did he speak like this to or about a child.

Significance of Jesus' attitude to children.

We have, then, two features of Jesus' ministry with regard to children to balance against each other. On the one hand he spoke quite surprisingly about the kingdom of God 'belonging' to children and about adults entering the kingdom of God only by becoming like little children. On the other hand he had no recorded ministry to children apart from their parents.

There are parallels between Jesus' approach to women and his approach to children. In both groups he was dealing with those who were marginalized in their society ('not counting the women and children', Matt.14:21). Jesus never condescended to either women or children, and never in the gospels do we find 'woman' or 'child' used as a term of disparagement, as they were, frequently, by many of his contemporaries, both Jewish and Gentile. But there are differences between his treatment of women and of children. Jesus spoke to women as he did to men; he numbered them among his followers, called them to discipleship. None of these things are said of children. He did not speak to them; he did not call them to discipleship. The coming of the kingdom of God did not make children into adults, but affirmed their childhood.

It was adults who were called to renounce self and possessions; rebuked for their lack of faith or spiritual blindness; summoned to faith and challenged to take up the cross. Adults, who we might think were complete and finished individuals, were called in the kingdom of God to become disciples, 'learners'. Children were not called to become learners in the kingdom, but rather were the model from which the adult learners could learn. Jesus affirmed what children were; but he challenged adults to become what they could be.

In the society of Jesus' day, children were perceived as embedded within the families to which they belonged. Jesus did not attempt to change that perception, or the position of children in his society. The kingdom of God did not mean some sort of Children's Crusade in which children were expected to take on adult roles. Because children were still children in the kingdom of God, and because Jesus affirmed them for what they were, they were not called out of their families, or forced into a kind of discipleship inappropriate to them and their status as children.

Jesus did enjoin on his followers a very special care and concern for children (Mk.9:42). He showed a remarkable amount of attention to children and clearly expected his disciples to do the same.

As Jesus' followers became the church and his band of disciples took an institutional form, one of the areas of greatest challenge would be their treatment of children. How would they remain faithful to the way Jesus had received the children and how would they express his affirmation of them? The answers to those questions are found in the story of children in the early church.

Chapter 3

Children in the Life of the Early Church

When Jesus's followers became a recognizable and organized movement in the first decades of the church's existence, they were faced with huge and momentous issues: their relationship with Judaism, from which they were emerging; the terms on which Gentiles could enter the movement; forms of leadership and the status and acceptability of particular prominent figures. Among the issues facing the infant church was that of what to do about children. But if we are to judge from the amount of written material dealing with children which we find in the New Testament letters and in the writings of the first couple of centuries of the church's life, we would have to say that it was not a problem which taxed the first Christians very greatly. Children and their place in the fellowship of Christians were not a focus of concern and discussion.

So, if we want to reconstruct a picture of the position of children in the early church, we have to recognise that in many areas we shall end up with more questions than answers. The surviving literature from the early church, both the letters of the New Testament and the writings of second and third century Christians, is largely problem-centred. It deals with matters which had become controversial or difficult for the Christian community. On no occasion did anyone in these early generations set out to write a complete account of Christian beliefs or a balanced compendium of Christian life and worship. So, in asking questions about the place of children in the church we are not going to find all the answers we might want (about infant baptism, for example) because we are posing questions about matters which do not seem to have been a problem to the earliest Christians, and therefore were not dealt with in the surviving literature.

This does not mean, though, that we can discover nothing at all about children in the early church, only that what we discover will be drawn from inferences or from passing references in our texts. In this chapter we shall look at the New Testament apart from the gospels, and see what we can discover from it about the place of children in the early church.

We shall explore something of the relationship between the home and the church, a relationship already hinted at in the last chapter where we examined Jesus's proclamation of a new community which called into question the absolute demands of the family and kinship group. We shall look at what people thought of children, as far as we can deduce this, and at what part children played in the life of the early church. We shall examine how children were treated by the church, what provision was made for their instruction in the Christian faith, and to what extent they participated in worship, and in the sacraments of baptism and the Eucharist. We shall extend our search for evidence beyond the New Testament itself to the first Christian generations after the New Testament period to see how the early Christians dealt with children. This has its own interest and has some light to throw, too, on the New Testament evidence.

Children in the New Testament Epistles

Words for 'child' or 'infant' occur quite frequently in the pages of the New Testament outside the gospels. But generally the authors of the letters in the New Testament were using the terms as descriptions of Christian believers, and frequently with an emphasis on their subjection to authority or with a reference to their immaturity in the faith.

Often the image of parent and child is used to describe the relationship between the writer of a letter and its recipients. In Paul's case, this image was expressing the fact that his missionary work had founded the congregation to which he was writing (1 Cor.4:14f., Gal.4:19, 1 Thess.2:11). Paul was the Corinthians' 'father' because the church had begun with his work in Corinth. No matter how many others may have had a hand in their upbringing, this basic fact could not be changed. Paul describes the other teachers and leaders as *paidagogoi*, the slave-custodians of small children whose role we examined in chapter one. Paul similarly describes Onesimus the runaway slave as his 'child', begotten, as Paul picturesquely puts it, in his chains – in other words, converted while Paul was a prisoner (Phm.10).

John uses diminutives, 'little children' (actually two different words in Greek: *teknion* and *paidion*) to address the recipients of his letter (1 Jn.2:1, 18, 28; 3:7, 18; 5:21). His choice of these diminutives expresses John's warm affection for those to whom he wrote. In 3 John 4 'my children' may indicate converts, or simply the writer's pastoral care for his readers. Used in this way, the imagery of Christians as children was drawing attention to the pattern of authority and care in the church. Paul or John stood as it were *in loco parentis* in their relationship with the churches to which they were writing. But the early Christians also used the comparison of Christian disciples with children to emphasize perceived immaturity in the congregations concerned.

It was this aspect of the child which seems to have most struck Paul, for instance. In one of his most celebrated passages, he uses the image of the child in this way: 'When I was a child I spoke like a child, thought like a child, reasoned like a child; but when I grew up I finished with childish things' (1 Cor.13:11).

In 1 Corinthians 13 his theme is the contrast between the partial grasp of the divine reality which we experience here and now, and that complete vision which will only be granted in the time to come. In this context, Paul writes of childhood as a phase of our living in which our life is incomplete, waiting the coming of wholeness and maturity which will only be attained in adulthood.

Elsewhere in the letters of the New Testament, infancy is drawn upon as a useful metaphor to combine notions of immaturity and lack of development. The baby or infant could be contrasted with the ideal of the fully formed adult, which was the ideal Christian disciples should be aiming for. In Ephesians, the goal of Christian discipleship is set as 'mature manhood, measured by nothing less than the full stature of Christ'. The opposite alternative is the status of children, 'tossed about by the waves and whirled around by every fresh gust of teaching, dupes of cunning rogues and their deceitful schemes' (Eph.4:13f.). Christian maturity is marked by a stability of life which is a recognizably adult characteristic.

In 1 Corinthians 3:1f., we find Paul upbraiding the Corinthians because they had failed to attain the spiritual maturity which Paul might have expected. So, as 'infants in Christ' they had to be fed on milk, not on solid food. Later in the same letter, he reverts to the theme: 'Do not be children in your thinking, my friends; be infants in evil, but in your thinking be grown-up' (1 Cor.14:20). The writer to the Hebrews used the same metaphor to criticize his readers' lack of progress in their understanding of the Christian faith. They were like unweaned infants; their diet had to be milk, which corresponded to a very basic level of Christian instruction, rather than solid food, which corresponded to more advanced teaching (Heb.5:12–14).

In 1 Corinthians and Hebrews the writers make plain that there is something disappointing about their readers' spiritual and personal development (1 Corinthians) or understanding of the faith (Hebrews). The comparison with infants or babies expresses criticism. But in 1 Peter we have a comparison which is not critical: 'Like the newborn infants you are, you should be craving for pure spiritual milk, so that you may thrive on it and be saved; for surely you have tasted that the Lord is good' (1 Pet.2:2f.).

Here in 1 Peter the writer makes a very positive comparison between the Christian believer and a baby. The 'milk' spoken of here is not, as with Hebrews, some form of elementary instruction from which the Christian convert quickly passes on to something stronger. Rather, it is that wholesome teaching, worship and encouragement which strengthens the Christian to live for Christ. And 1 Peter speaks of the baby, not as an example of a stage of life soon (and rightly) to be left behind, but as an example of natural and insatiable appetite.

Interestingly, no New Testament writer makes any reference to the innocence of children, a favourite theme in the surrounding culture and a quality frequently mentioned in epitaphs, in particular. Christian writers in the second century argued that the absolute cleansing of forgiveness in Christ could be compared to a return to the innocency of childhood (*Letter of Barnabas* 6.11), or that believers who achieve moral perfection are like children in their purity of life (*Shepherd of Hermas*, Mandate 2.1, Similitude 9.29). Such ideas are absent from the New Testament letters. Paul, writing of 'your children' as 'holy' evidently meant some quality conferred on children (and spouses) by their connection with the Christian community. The New Testament does not contain any idealizing of the moral state of childhood.

So we find in the letters of the New Testament a contrast with the teaching of Jesus on children and discipleship. Jesus took the child as an example for the disciple, as well as commending children to the disciples' particular care. Jesus invited his followers to look at children with new eyes. The writers of the New Testament letters used the image of the child in their description of discipleship in much more conventional ways. For them, children were persons under the authority of parents, ready examples of immaturity and of potential for growth. All of these are quite legitimate ways of viewing children, but each one corresponds to the accepted perception of the children in society, rather than, as with Jesus, challenging that perception.

Children in the Life of the Early Church

It is not easy to form a clear picture of exactly what it was like to take part in the worship of the early church. Here and there we have glimpses, as with the freedom of the Corinthians in 1 Corinthians 14:26–40 or the night-time meeting of the church at Troas in Acts 20:7–12. We can make more or less informed guesses about what may have been carried over from the worship of the synagogue, or where the celebration of the Lord's Supper may have fitted in. Occasionally we have the witness of an outsider such as the younger Pliny, who, as governor of Bithynia in Asia Minor, sent a report of what he could discover concerning the Christians in his province to the Emperor Trajan around the year 112 AD (Pliny, *Letters* 10.96: *NE* 18–20).

In all likelihood, worship took different forms in different places, and at any one time we would probably find a wide mix of freedom and order in worship. What Christians did when they came together was probably also changing quite rapidly in the first few generations. We cannot therefore suppose that the pattern of Christian worship was fixed and unvarying either from place to place, or over time.

If we could eavesdrop on a Christian meeting for worship in the late first century, it seems very probable, for all the difference and diversity between one place and another, that we would have found children present. Luke says as much in the book of Acts. In Acts 20:7–12, we read of the hapless young man called Eutychus, who chose the wrong place to sit at a Communion service in Troas. It was held in an upper room on the evening of the first day of the week (either Saturday or Sunday, depending on whether Luke was using Jewish or Roman reckoning). Unfortunately for Eutychus, it was to be Paul's last visit to Troas, and perhaps because there was a large congregation gathered to hear the apostle, Eutychus sat on a window ledge. Quite certainly, Paul took the opportunity to pack as much as possible into the evening, because Luke tells us that the service eventually lasted all night. Eutychus, overcome by sleep, fell out of the window and was taken for dead. Paul, throwing himself Elijah-like upon him, reassured the congregation that he was alive. Luke describes Eutychus as 'a young man' and as 'a boy' (Acts 20:9, 12). It is difficult to be specific about how old Luke thought Eutychus was. Probably the English 'youth' would cover the age range which Luke had in mind.

Younger children are mentioned at Tyre, where the wives and children joined the male disciples in kneeling in worship on the beach at Paul's departure from the city (Acts. 21:5). An early manuscript (Codex Bezae, fifth century) adds children to the picture of the first church in Jerusalem. In Acts 1:14, it reads: 'All these with one accord were constantly at prayer, together with a group of women *and children*'. It is unlikely that the words 'and children' come from Luke. Probably an early scribe added them. But they do show that Christians in the early church, like that scribe, expected children to be present at worship.

Pliny said of the people of Bithynia during his governorship (c.112 AD) that 'many of all ages' were in danger of contagion from the Christian menace (Pliny, *Letter* 10.96.9: *NE* 19). He had evidently noticed that children were involved in the Christian worship which he was trying to stamp out in his province. Cyprian (Bishop of Carthage, d.258 AD), wrote in his book *On the Lapsed*, of a mother bringing her child to the Eucharist (*On the Lapsed* 25). There is no doubt that children were present at worship in the New Testament period, and continued to be present in succeeding generations of the church. It is less clear precisely what their status was and what significance was attached to their presence. How far were they regarded as part of the congregation and how far were they there merely out of necessity? This question has to be be answered, partly, by looking at baptism and the Eucharist, as we shall do in the next chapter. But we do have some evidence apart from that which relates to the sacraments.

Paul mentions the status of children in households where one partner was a Christian, and the other was not. He states in 1 Corinthians 7:14 that 'your children (presumably the children of the whole Christian community) belong to God' (literally 'are holy'). He states this, not as a problem, but as an established and agreed point,which applies even when only one partner is a Christian. It seems to be a matter of family solidarity that one parent being 'holy', (a Christian), affects the status of the children, and even the status of the other spouse ('For the husband now belongs to God through his Christian wife, and the wife through her Christian husband'). This verse is a difficult one for the modern reader. But the point for our purposes is that Paul counts the children as *in* the community of faith, not out of it. So that when children came to worship, even if they came from a household where only one parent was a believer, they came as part of the church, as participants in worship, not as mere observers.

We may doubt, though, whether New Testament worship was 'all-age worship' in the sense in which services in our own day try to involve worshippers of all ages. Certainly, Paul's Communion service at Troas did not make any concessions to the young! To come back to a passage which has been mentioned before, in Matthew 14:21, at the end of the feeding of the five thousand: 'Some five thousand men shared in this meal, not counting women and children'. Here again the children were present – and incidentally, John calls attention to their presence by identifying the source of the loaves and fishes as 'a boy' (Jn.6:9). But these words of Matthew express an attitude towards children: the 'real' participants in the miracle are the men, with the women and children being seen as peripheral. In this, Matthew is no doubt echoing the social perceptions of his time. Equally, Matthew is likely to be expressing the perceptions of the church of which he was a part. The feeding of the five thousand is a story with obvious Eucharistic overtones (most clearly exploited by John in the sixth chapter of his gospel). In the gathering of the men, with the women and children, to be fed by Jesus, we cannot help seeing a parallel with the gathering of the church for the breaking of the bread. The place of the children at the miracle (present but marginal), may tell us something indirectly about their place in the church as Matthew knew it.

We have to recall that the first Christians had no separate church buildings in which to meet. When they came together it was in the homes of the church's members (see, for example, Rom.16:5 with reference to Prisca and Aquila: 'Greet also the church that meets at their house'). Inevitably, the host's children, if any, would be there when the church gathered for worship and teaching. Many Christians were people of low social status, hence the choice of early morning or late evening for their time of worship – it was the only time that they might be free from work. We can well imagine such people bringing the whole family with them to the home where they were to worship together.

To some extent the presence of children in the worship of the first Christians was therefore a matter of necessity. But Paul's acceptance of the children of the church as 'belonging to God' or 'holy' suggests that the children were not only there because they had to be. They were there because they belonged there. We gain the impression that their presence did not significantly alter the form of worship, and that they were rather on the edge of things, but that is not the whole picture. We need next to ask more positively what the early church did for children or with them, what provision was made for their instruction or education in the Christian faith. That is the theme of our next section.

Christian education of the young

In the early church we find a tension between church and family as the location for the instruction and education of children in the faith.

Without stretching our slim evidence too far, we can trace a tendency in the first Christian generations to delegate the task of bringing children up in the Christian way to the family, and to fathers in particular.

We have already seen Paul's insistence, in 1 Corinthians 7:14, that the child of a believing parent 'belongs to God' or 'is holy'. The corollary of this is that children took their place in the church alongside adults. If that was the case, then we would expect children to be addressed in the letters of the New Testament, together with the adults. In some letters this does in fact happen.

We should set aside John's address to 'children' in 1 John 2:12f., 'I write to you, children, because your sins have been forgiven for his sake . . . I have written to you, children, because you know the Father'. From the context, in a letter in which he describes all Christians as 'children', it is most likely that in this passage, too, John means all Christians or perhaps specifically the young in the faith.

But in the closely-related letters of Colossians and Ephesians we have two significant passages where children are spoken to:

> Children, obey your parents [in the Lord]; for it is only right that you should. 'Honour your father and your mother' is the first commandment to carry a promise with it: 'that it may be well with you and that you may live long on the earth'. Fathers, do not goad your children to resentment, but bring them up in the discipline and instruction of the Lord. (Eph.6:1–4)

> Children, obey your parents in everything, for that is pleasing to God and is the Christian way. Fathers, do not exasperate your children, in case they lose heart. (Col.3:20f.)

The content of these instructions reinforces the normal social position of children, enjoining obedience and respect for parents. But more remarkable is the fact that these instructions exist at all. In each letter they are found in a list of ethical instructions to people in different positions within the household. Such lists exist in other New Testament letters, and indeed outside the New Testament as well. They were a common form of ethical instruction. The unique feature of these lists in Ephesians and Colossians is that children feature in the groups to which instruction is given.

The letters of the New Testament were not written for individual study, but to be read to the congregation, as we are reminded by Colossians 4:16: 'Once this letter has been read among you, see that it is read also to the church at Laodicea, and that you in turn read my letter to Laodicea'. Each group in these ethical lists – husbands, wives, children and slaves – was addressed because these people were present in the meeting for worship and would hear the letter being read out. The mention of children in Colossians and Ephesians is therefore not only an acknowledgement that children were attending worship, as we have seen was the case from other evidence, but also that there were instruction and teaching included specifically for them. It seems likely that what was said in Colossians and Ephesians would be copied by those who taught the congregations on other occasions – the prophets, evangelists, pastors and teachers mentioned in Eph.4:11 – and we can imagine such ministers themselves addressing part of their message to children.

In at least some congregations, therefore, children were not merely passive spectators on the edge of what was going on, but were taught and encouraged alongside the adults during the course of the church's meeting for worship. It was acknowledged that much of their nurture in the Christian faith would happen in the home, and Ephesians in particular mentions the father's role in this respect: 'Fathers, do not goad your children to resentment, but bring them up in the discipline and instruction of the Lord' (Eph.6:4). But children's presence at worship was recognized by including material for them in the congregation's teaching. Significantly also, Colossians and Ephesians make the responsibilities of parents and children mutual. If children owe their parents the duty of respect, no less do parents owe their children the duty of consideration. This was quite a radical idea in the culture of the time, where a far more one-way relationship would be the norm. The commandment quoted in Ephesians 6:2, 'Honour your father and your mother', enjoined the normal social respect for parents. Ephesians does nothing to undermine this respect; it builds it into a wider vision of a family which can be a living expression of life in Christ. So here the relationship of parents and children is part of the mutual concern characteristic of all Christian living, which is profoundly and simply set out in Ephesians by the maxim at the head of its ethical list: 'Be subject to one another out of reverence for Christ' (Eph.5:21). Some manuscripts include the words 'in the Lord' in Ephesians 6:1. Modern translators have taken different views about the authenticity of these words, some including them, and others excluding them from their translations. But if authentic, the phrase 'obey your parents in the Lord' would certainly underline the theme of the whole passage: that the mutual submission of members of the household is something only realised as they are all 'in Christ'.

Jesus, in his ministry, had called his followers into a new community in which the demands and expectations of family life were no longer absolute, but moulded by the demands of the kingdom, as we saw in the previous chapter. In chapter one we saw something of the heavy-handed discipline of the first-century home. Colossians and Ephesians challenged the widespread assumption that the parental role carried with it an unlimited authority over the children of the family. Christian discipleship set limits to the exercise of parental authority and discipline – 'Fathers, do not goad your children to resentment'.

Here in Colossians and Ephesians, we see a practical expression of Jesus' vision for the family and the kingdom of God. Here the family is no longer an autocratic institution, but a place for all members to grow together in their common life in Christ. Something similar could be said about the way the relationship of masters and slaves is made mutual in Colossians and Ephesians (Col.3:22–4.1, Eph.6:5–9).

In the churches addressed by Colossians and Ephesians, children were in evidence as members of the congregation. In other congregations, however, children seem not to have been so clearly part of the church's worshipping life. The three letters known as the Pastoral Epistles (1 & 2 Timothy and Titus) appear to take a rather different approach to the place of children in the Christian community. In Titus 2:1–10 we have a list of ethical instructions similar to those in Colossians and Ephesians, but with some differences, of which the most conspicuous is the omission of children. If we ask why the children have dropped from view, the answer seems to be that they have been relegated to the domestic sphere, and responsibility for teaching them delegated to parents, and to mothers in particular.

In 1 Timothy 3:4f. we are told that the bishop or overseer must control his children without losing his dignity, and that the way he manages his household is a mark of his ability to manage a congregation. A similar quality is also required in a deacon (1 Tim.3:12), and, as Titus lays down, in an elder (Tit.1:6). Here the emphasis seems to fall, more emphatically than in Colossians or Ephesians, on a family which is governed by the father, and on children as objects of paternal control. In these letters the emphasis is on the control of young people so that the household, and the household of faith, will not lose face in the wider community. In later Christian literature, the same theme of the control of young people will be repeated, with emphasis shifted to concern for the young person's salvation.

These letters have a distinctive and characteristic concern for the church as a household. 1 Timothy 3:15 describes the church as 'God's household', and the Pastoral Epistles consistently call for a church life built upon skilfully-managed households; for a church which is itself organized on the pattern of an orderly household (see Verner 1983). The church and the Christian households which made up the church, were exhorted to exhibit a subordination of young to old; women to men; slaves to masters. The maintenance of this ideal is portrayed in the Pastoral Epistles as largely a problem of management: the older were responsible for the behaviour of the younger, men for the women, adults for the children, and the leadership of the church for its members. It is significant that the letters themselves are in the form of an address to church leaders, rather than to the whole congregation.

In the Pastoral Epistles, men are made responsible for the public face of the household, as it were, and women for its internal life. Young women are exhorted to motherhood (Tit.2:4). 1 Timothy states: 'Salvation for the woman will be in the bearing of children, provided she continues in faith, love, and holiness, with modesty' (1 Tim.2:15). It is one of the New Testament's most puzzling statements, but probably the meaning is that if a woman gives her attention fully to her proper role of bearing children, she will be in a more spiritually safe position than Eve, whose temptation and fall brought down Adam with her (1 Tim.2:12f.), or than those young widows, 'gossips and busybodies', who have 'taken the wrong turning and gone over to Satan' (1 Tim.5:11–15). The right course for a young widow, 1 Timothy says, is to remarry, have children, and manage a household (1 Tim.5:14). Children, in the Pastoral Epistles, are the woman's business.

The woman's responsibility for her children could extend to bringing them up in the faith and teaching them to know and love the scriptures, perhaps especially if her husband was an unbeliever. So it happened to Timothy, who was made familiar from childhood with the scriptures, presumably by his mother and grandmother (2 Tim.1:5, 3:14f.; his father did not share the faith of his mother, Acts 16:1).

Children's discipleship, which was given its own place in Colossians and Ephesians, was absent from the Pastoral Epistles. Children have become part of their parents' discipleship; they make their appearance only on the margin as objects of control and as problems requiring proper management. The Pastoral Epistles envisage predominantly one-way relationships, in which the socially superior (elder, male, master) takes responsibility for the conduct of the inferior (younger, female, slave). The mutuality of relationships which we saw in Colossians and Ephesians is replaced here by management of relationships.

It is often remarked by commentators that the Pastoral Epistles conform to the received ethical opinions and dominant social expectations of the surrounding culture of the day. This appears to be true of the place of children in these letters, and in the church as they describe it. We could characterize the difference between Ephesians on the one hand and the Pastoral Epistles on the other by saying that, while the Pastoral Epistles take the ideal ancient household as the model for the church (1 Tim.3:15), Ephesians takes the church as the body of Christ to be the model of the household and family (Eph.3:14-19). Of the two ways of understanding the Christian family, it was that of the Pastoral Epistles which predominated in early Christianity. In consequence, we find that children practically vanish from the church's concern. After Colossians and Ephesians, children were occasionally spoken *about*, but never spoken *to*.

In the post-New Testament period, the tendency continues of delegating to the family the task of teaching children in the faith. In the First Letter of Clement, written from Rome to Corinth about 96 AD, Clement speaks directly to the men of the congregation about their responsibilities: 'Let us instruct the young in the fear of God, let us lead our wives to what is good . . . Let our children share in the instruction which is in Christ' (*1 Clem.* 26.6 and 8). Both women and children have ceased to be instructed directly in the church, and are to be instructed and directed by the father and husband.

The *Didache*, or *Teaching of the Apostles* (date uncertain, but probably early second century) speaks to parents about the need not to 'withold your hand' [in punishment] from your son or daughter, but to bring them up in the fear of the Lord (*Didache* 4.9). Polycarp, Bishop of Smyrna (c.69–c.155), wrote to the Philippians with moral instruction which, like Clement's before him, spoke to the men about how they were to instruct their wives. Among the wife's duties was 'to educate the children in the education of the fear of God' (Polycarp, *Philippians* 4.2). In this post-New Testament material we trace the shape of a church made up of households as their basic building block. Within these households the husbands and fathers were in charge, and through them moral and other guidance was mediated to the rest of the family. This hierarchical order conformed to the cultural expectation of the times. It was one of the points in favour of the church which Aristides could point to in his defence of Christians, written some time in the early to mid-second century: 'As for their [the Christians'] servants or handmaids, or their children, if any of them have any, they persuade them to become Christians for the love that they have towards them; and when they have become so, they call them without distinction brethren' (*Apology* 15.6: *NE* 53). This picture of the pastoral care of the *paterfamilias* extending over his servants and children was one which contemporaries could understand. Aristides drew attention to this feature of Christian domestic life to help clear Christians of the charge of the dangerous and anti-social radicalism which outsiders feared from this community of 'brothers'.

We could ask what difference it made to a child or young person to be brought up within a Christian rather than a pagan home. At the start of life, the Christian child, like his or her Jewish contemporary, would have greater protection from the danger of infanticide, which, as we saw in chapter one, was a widespread practice in the ancient world (above, pp.3-5,21f.). The *Didache*, which was written to instruct Christian converts in the basic moral expectations of their new-found faith, spells out Christian instruction in this area: 'You shall not kill a child in the womb, nor shall you slay it when born' (*Did.* 2.2). In the mid-second century, Justin Martyr wrote a vehement diatribe against infant exposure and its attendant evils, claiming it as one of the virtues of the Christians that they did not expose the newborn (*1 Apology 27*). Like Philo before him (see p.4f.), Justin played on an unspoken disquiet in the pagan world.

In the matter of discipline, both heavy-handed and lenient regimes were experienced by Christian children. But some Christian authors interestingly reinterpreted the idea of discipline, understanding it not so much as a matter of physical beating, as of personal formation, and substituting words for blows as a means of correction and guidance. Here is the advice of the so-called *Teaching of the Apostles* (*Didascalia Apostolorum*), a Syrian Christian church order of the early third century, on the subject of disciplining children:

> Do not hesitate to reprove them [your children], reasoning with them and chastising them and arguing; for you will not kill them by chastising them, but rather give them life, as also our Lord teaches us in wisdom, saying: Chastise your son, since thus is his hope; beat him with a rod, you will free his soul from hell [Prov.29:17; 25:14]. Our 'rod' is the word of Jesus Christ, as Jeremiah saw a branch of an almond tree [Jer.1:11]. Everyone therefore who hesitates to speak a word of chastisement to his son, hates his son. (*Didascalia* 4.11; Funk 1906 1 230,232)

Christian writers in the early centuries urged on their readers the duty of exercising parental control over their children well into adolescence. By contrast, in pagan circles, the pseudo-Plutarch (see above, p.33) advised turning a diplomatic blind eye to adolescent extravagance:

> I do not think they [fathers] should be utterly harsh and austere in their nature, but they should in many cases concede some shortcomings to the younger person, and remind themselves that they were once young . . . It is a good thing also to pretend not to know of some shortcomings, and to turn the old man's dull eye and dull ear to what they do, and, seeing, not to see, and hearing, not hear, sometimes, what goes on . . . In this fashion is restive youth gradually broken to harness. (pseudo-Plutarch, *Education* 18)

But no Christian author took such an easygoing attitude to the upbringing of the young. Too much, they believed, was at stake: not merely a young person's happiness but their eternal destiny. They consistently urged on parents the tight control of children which we have already seen in the Pastoral Epistles (above, pp.75-7). John Chrysostom used the image of making a beautiful statue. Christian parents are responsible for a work of grace far more significant than the most beautiful work of art, and the care they take of their children should be still greater than the love a sculptor lavishes on his creation. Chrysostom particularly said that the adolescent boy (his main, though not exclusive concern) should be kept away from public places, mixed bathing, and theatres (*Vainglory* 56, 60, 77–9). The *Teaching of the Apostles* also saw spiritual danger in the universal youthful habit of simply going about together:

> And they [young people] shall do nothing without your consent, nor should they go out with their peers, to get together and enjoy themselves, for thus they learn foolishness, and are captured by fornication, and fall. (*Didascalia* 4.11.4, Funk 1906 1 232)

Both the *Teaching of the Apostles* in the third century, writing for rank-and-file Christians and John Chrysostom in the fourth century, writing for the social élite, advised early arranged marriages in order to avoid temptations to sin (*Didascalia 4.11*, Funk 1906 1 232; Vainglory 81f.).

Christians and Pagan Education

The early Christians lived in a society whose values were inimical to them in many respects. The pagan society around them was underpinned by a religion which they considered false, if not demonic; it was characterized by moral values they could not share; and it was entered into by an education steeped in paganism. So we might expect the early Christians to try to protect their young people by providing some alternative form of education which would keep them free from the temptations and snares of the pagan world in which they lived. They had, after all, the example of the Jewish synagogue schools. But, rather surprisingly, the Christians did not take that course for several centuries. There was no fiercer critic of paganism than Tertullian (c.160–c.225), but even he accepted the necessity for young people to share in the education on offer at pagan schools. His chosen image to describe the Christian pupil's situation as he read the pagan authors whose work formed the ancient syllabus, was that of someone offered poison to drink, but refusing to take it (*On Idolatry* 10).

The young Origen (born c.185 AD), who was to grow up to be one of the church's most brilliant and controversial theologians, is said to have received extra instruction in the Scriptures from his father, Leonides, each day before he set out for his secular schooling (Eusebius, *Ecclesiastical History* 6.2.7f.). This is an interesting picture of Christian education at the close of the second century. Even if the story is a pious legend, it still shows us what Christians thought that a conscientious Christian ought to do about his children's education. Here was a devout Christian father, later to be martyred for the gospel, who was nonetheless willing for his son to attend school, and follow the normal curriculum of the pagan classics. Origen's home was the great city of Alexandria, but even there, it seems, there was no provision for Christian children to be taught in a specifically Christian school. By about the year 200, Alexandria was unique in having a Christian catechetical school, which Origen later attended. But the harm, from a Christian point of view, had already been done in the early education of children in the pagan classics, before ever they reached the more advanced work which might be done in the catechetical school. Origen himself became an enthusiast for secular education as a preparation for Biblical study, and in later life urged it on those who came to him for instruction (Eusebius, *Ecclesiastical History* 6.18.4: *NE* 192).

We hear of no Christian schooling outside the home in the early centuries. A century after Clement had written to Corinthian fathers and husbands to 'instruct the young in the fear of God', the same pattern of family responsibility can be seen in Origen's Alexandria. Christian parents were still content for their children to share a common education with their pagan neighbours, and the church was slow to copy the the synagogue in providing an alternative pattern of schooling. Even when John Chrysostom (c.347–407) wrote the first Christian treatise on the education of children (*On the Vainglory of the World and on the Education of Children*), he addressed himself to parents, and said nothing about sending children to specifically Christian schools. The first Christian schools seem to have been those founded by the monasteries from the fourth century onwards (Marrou 1965 472–84).

It is worth asking why Christians did not take the opportunity to create their own schools. If we take the comparison with the Jewish community, one reason must have been that there was no need for Christian children to learn a sacred language; their Jewish contemporaries had to learn Hebrew. Those who spoke Greek could read the New Testament in its original language, and the Old Testament in Greek translation. And the New Testament Scriptures were rapidly translated into the various languages of the Mediterranean. Further, Christians did not see themselves as culturally distinct from their neighbours. An anonymous writer of the late second century expressed eloquently how Christians were in the world, but not of it:

> For Christians are not distinguished from the rest of mankind by country, or by speech, or by dress. For they do not dwell in cities of their own, or use a different language, or practise a peculiar life . . . But while they dwell in Greek or barbarian cities according as each man's lot has been cast, and follow the customs of the land in clothing and food, and other matters of daily life, yet the condition of citizenship which they exhibit is wonderful, and admittedly strange . . . Every foreign land is to them a fatherland, and every fatherland a foreign land. (*Epistle to Diognetus* 6.1–5: *NE* 55).

To set up their own separate educational provision would have been to withdraw from the common life they shared with their pagan neighbours. And, while they recognized the dangers and allure of paganism, the early Christians saw no need to do that. They let their children 'share in the instruction which is in Christ' (1 Clement), and they allowed them access to education for the wider pagan society. They were not trying to create a Christian ghetto, but to be salt and light in their world. Their attitude to their children's education was an expression of this open yet critical attitude.

Children in the Christian Household

The churches of the second century were networks of patriarchal households of the sort which Aristides portrayed, and to which Ignatius of Antioch wrote around 100 AD: 'I salute the families (or households) of my brethren with their wives and children, and the maidens called widows' (Ignatius, *Smyrnaeans* 13.1). Ignatius exactly summarizes the situation. The church's front rank was composed of the 'brethren' to whom its constituent households belonged. Under them were the women and children, with the 'widows' (perhaps an order in the church) as a separate category. The church had found a form in which it could survive and even prosper in the society of its day, but at the cost of some aspects of mutual submission and responsibility as voiced in Colossians and Ephesians.

The modern observer is likely to have little sympathy with what can be seen of the way in which the second-century church treated its women and children members. The emergence of the patriarchal structure which we see in the writings of the Apostolic Fathers (Clement, Polycarp, Ignatius) may look, from our point of view, like a decline – both from the teaching and example of Jesus and from the insights of Paul about the child's inclusion among God's people.

But before we dismiss the course taken by the church, we should bear two things in mind. The first is that the church adopted a form of existence which would allow it to work with the grain of the surrounding culture, which, as we saw in chapter one, was markedly patriarchal. This adaptation, which seems to have been well under way by the time the Pastoral Epistles were written, was perhaps a necessary evolution for the church to maintain its witness. Further, as a matter of principle, we recall that Jesus' own ministry to children was through their parents. The second century church was therefore developing in a line with the precedent of Jesus's own ministry.

The second point to bear in mind is that provision for instruction and education of children in the church, at least for the first few generations, was seen to be important. When children are mentioned in early Christian literature, it is relatively often in the context of bringing them up in the faith. Consequently, though we know little enough of how the church set about the task of nurturing children in the faith, the little we know is at least more than we know about, for instance, whether children were baptized, a subject on which the earliest sources are silent. And we would have to say that the system, such as it was, worked. The church grew not only by evangelism but by biological growth, as successive generations accepted the faith of Christ. Justin Martyr, writing a defence of Christianity around 155 AD, could point to 'many men and women of sixty and seventy years of age, who became disciples of Christ from their childhood' (*1 Apology* 1.15). The saintly Polycarp declared at his martyrdom (also c.155 AD) that he was one of those who had been a Christian from childhood: 'For eighty-six years I have been Christ's servant and he has done me no wrong, and how can I blaspheme my King who saved me?' (*Martyrdom of Polycarp* 9.3: *NE* 25). In 165 AD Justin went to his martyrdom. He was a convert in adulthood, but among those who perished with him were Euelpistus and Paeon, both of whom declared that they had received their Christian faith, or 'the good confession', from their parents (*Acts of St. Justin and his companions* 4: *NE* 33). By the middle of the second century there were many men and women who had been brought up in the church. Cradle Christians, as well as converts, were to be found in the ranks of the martyrs.

Chapter 4

Children and the Sacraments

We have seen that children were present in Christian worship from the earliest days, and that some attention was given to bringing them up and instructing them in the Christian faith. But what was their status in the congregation? Were they baptized? Were they admitted to the Lord's Supper? The issue of baptism, in particular, has enormous divisive potential for Christians today. It is the only aspect of the place of children in the New Testament church which has generated any substantial interest among modern-day Christians.

Children and Baptism

This issue has explosive potential for us largely because, paradoxically, it was so unimportant for the early church. If any person in the first two centuries of the church had taken the trouble to state plainly whether or not children or infants were suitable candidates for baptism, then an enormous quantity of ink could have been saved, and the church could have been spared a divisive and troublesome controversy. But the policy of 'not counting the children' extended to this vital area of initiation, also, leaving us today regrettably ill-informed about whether or not children were baptized by the early Christians.

Several major works on baptism have been published in recent decades. Some have argued passionately for the New Testament origin of infant baptism (Jeremias 1960 1963, Green 1987). Others have argued equally firmly that the baptism of infants was, historically speaking, an innovation of the third century, and in theological terms is a misunderstanding of the meaning of baptism as the New Testament presents it (Aland 1963, Beasley-Murray 1972). Still others have attempted to adjudicate the debate (Yates 1993). Various churches and denominations have produced reports on Christian initiation, which have of necessity touched on this subject. But for all the attention given to the topic, it would have to be said that we are no nearer a resolution of the argument than when the Anabaptists of the sixteenth century were arguing with Zwingli, Calvin and the other magisterial Reformers.

Where evidence is so slight, dogmatism is clearly out of place. In the following pages we will attempt to look at the evidence, building on what we have seen of the education and instruction of the young in the early church, to try and frame an answer two questions, one historical and one theological. Did the early church baptize infants? And does the New Testament evidence on baptism exclude or encourage the baptism of children or infants?

A Practice Without a Doctrine

If we start with the historical aspect of the matter, we have to recognize that we cannot tell the story of the development of baptism with regard to children as a continuous narrative because we have so little solid evidence to go on. So the usual maxim about beginning at the beginning does not apply here. We will do better in this instance to start with what is known, beginning with the period in which we can see clearly, and then work back to the unknown in the earlier centuries.

The early third century is the first point at which we can start to see what was happening with regard to children and baptism. Before 200 AD we have no references to baptism which give us much help in deciding whether or not children were being baptized. The clearest evidence from the second century, such as it is, comes from the Christian apologist Aristides (probably mid-century) who wrote:

> Now they [the Christians] persuade the servants and maids, if they have any, or the children, that they become Christians, because of the love which they have for them. And when they have become Christians, they call them 'brothers' without distinction. (Aristides, *Apology* 15.6: *NE* 53).

Aristides could mean that the children of Christian homes were only baptized ('became Christians') when they were old enough to be 'persuaded'. But the reference to 'children' here is rather problematic. Are we meant to think that Christian parents called their children 'brothers'? And why should Aristides mention the Christian householder's own children as a clumsy afterthought behind the slaves? Jeremias was probably right to argue that the 'children' here were the children of the slaves, and that the male and female household slaves were being 'persuaded' to become Christians, and that they were the ones who, once persuaded to become Christians, were then called brothers (Jeremias 1963 43–8).

The second century is rather uninformative, but from the start of the third century a small number of sources begin to speak about the baptism of infants or children. The earliest of these sources is Tertullian, writing in North Africa around 200 AD. Tertullian knew about the baptism of small children, but was unhappy about it. Those who favoured the baptism of infants apparently appealed to Matthew 19.14: 'Let the children come to me; do not try to stop them'. Tertullian wanted to tackle them on their own ground, and wrest this text from them:

> The Lord indeed says, 'Forbid them not to come unto me'. Let them come, then, while they are learning, while they are being taught whither to come; let them become Christians when they have been able to know Christ. Why hurries the age of innocence to the remission of sins? (Tertullian *On Baptism* 18: *NE* 173)

Tertullian's words immediately pose a difficulty for us. What was Tertullian doing? Was he championing an established custom, the baptism of young people at years of discretion and not before, against an innovation, that is, the baptism of infants? Or conversely, was he challenging the existing custom of infant baptism, and calling on the church to postpone baptism to a later stage than had been usual? Was he the upholder of the primitive Christian baptismal policy, or a radical innovator? Unfortunately for our purposes, his words do not make this clear, and modern interpreters have taken his meaning in both ways.

We shall have to reconsider the answer to this problem when we have more parts of the puzzle assembled. But to put his remarks in context, we should note that Tertullian feared that baptismal candidates were being committed to a standard of life which they might be unable to maintain. Like all early Christians, he took very seriously the problem of forgiveness of sins committed after baptism (Tertullian, *On Repentance*, 7.9: *NE* 174f.), and he was therefore arguing in his work *On Baptism* that the rite should not be administered hastily. He had to deal with instances of 'rash' baptisms in the New Testament, such as Philip's baptism of the Ethiopian in Acts 8, in order to show that these cases did not undermine his argument. Having dealt with possible scriptural objections to what he was arguing, Tertullian turned to consider what classes of person would not be suitable candidates for baptism. Children, we have seen, were one such group, but he had the same concern about baptizing unmarried persons. Until their way of life had settled either into marriage or confirmed chastity they were in an uncertain state and were not proper subjects for baptism (Tertullian, *On Baptism* 18: *NE* 174). There is no reason to suppose that Tertullian was defending an established custom of postponing the baptism of the unmarried. Rather, he seems to be urging a change of policy to take account of the seriousness of post-baptismal sin. Could it be that his argument against the baptism of small children was also his own idea, running counter to the practice of the church of his day? His appeal, after all, was to *principle*, as he interpreted it, and not to the practice which he knew.

There is one aspect of the practice of baptism, which Tertullian knew, which is hard to explain on the assumption that infant baptism was an innovation. Tertullian wrote of the 'sponsors' of infant candidates for baptism, and the spiritual danger they were in by committing themselves to the infant, who was a spiritually unkown quantity. So the baptismal rite known to Tertullian included sponsors or godparents for the infant candidates, and he could introduce them into his argument without having to explain who they were or what they did. If the baptism of infants was indeed an innovation in Tertullian's day, it was well-enough established to have some settled features, and for everyone likely to read Tertullian's words to know what a 'sponsor' was, without being told.

Also in North Africa, and contemporary with Tertullian, we have the evidence of the *Martyrdom of Saints Perpetua and Felicitas*, which has already been mentioned in chapter one (p.8f.). Perpetua, a young Christian woman imprisoned and awaiting execution (probably in 203 AD) for her refusal to sacrifice to the emperor, wrote an account of her tribulations and her visions in the text now known as the *Martyrdom*. Perpetua already had a baby and, while she herself was baptized in prison, nothing is said of the child's baptism (*Martyrdom* 3). Similarly Felicitas gave birth in prison and, again, nothing is said of her baby's baptism (*Martyrdom* 15). Aland took this as evidence that infant baptism was still unkown in the African church at the start of the third century.

But like so much of the debate about infant baptism in the early church, we have an argument from silence here. The two children may have been baptized without its being mentioned. But even supposing that we take the text's silence as an indication that the children were not baptized, what is the significance of this? The most recent editor of the *Martyrdom* has suggested that its author and her circle were strongly influenced by the Montanist movement, which also influenced Tertullian himself (Musurillo 1972 xxvi). The *Martyrdom* is not, therefore, an independent witness. It has to be seen as evidence that Tertullian was not merely speaking for himself when he stated his reservations about infant baptism, but was putting the views of a wider circle of Christians in North Africa. The *Martyrdom* does not help us decide the most important question of whether Tertullian and his circle were innovators or conservatives regarding infant baptism.

After Tertullian, the next evidence comes from Hippolytus, writing in Rome shortly after 200 AD. His *Apostolic Tradition* gives a fascinating and important picture of worship, as he knew it, in Rome in the early years of the third century. When he describes baptism, he states that the first to be baptized in any group of candidates were the children:

> First, the little ones should be baptized. All who can speak for themselves should speak. For those, however, who cannot, their parents or another who belongs to the family should speak (Hippolytus, *Apostolic Tradition* 21.3f. The text in *NE* 141–3 follows the Latin version in omitting this passage, see the following paragraph).

This statement sounds clear enough. But unfortunately there are difficulties even with this apparently clear piece of evidence. The original Greek version of Hippolytus' work has been lost and it now exists only in the form of translations into Latin and other languages. The Latin version (which seems to be the earliest and most reliable) does not include this section on children's baptism. Aland therefore suggested that it was not an original part of Hippolytus' work as he wrote it, but was added by later copyists who were familiar with the practice of infant baptism, and thought that there should be some mention of it in the text (Aland 1963 49f.). However, this passage about the baptism of the infants is present in other versions of the *Apostolic Tradition*, and many scholars are content to accept it as original. So Hippolytus is probably a witness to the baptism of infants at Rome in the very early third century, but his evidence has to be used with caution.

The next evidence comes from Egypt, where Origen (c.185–c.254) described the baptism of infants as a tradition of the church (*In Lev.Hom.* 8.3), received from the apostles (*Commentary on Romans* 5.9). This is a very significant testimony. Unlike Tertullian, Origen is witnessing to the custom of the church, and not merely expressing his own views. Unlike Hippolytus, there is no question about the authenticity of his words.

Origen could, of course, have been wrong about the apostolic origins of infant baptism. He was writing, it must be recalled, the best part of two centuries after the time of the apostles, and not all rites which people in Origen's time claimed to have received from the apostles were in fact

apostolic in origin. But Origen was a well-travelled man. By the time that
he wrote in his *Commentary on Romans* that infant baptism had been
received from the apostles, Origen had lived in Palestine as well as his
native Egypt, and he had visited both Rome and Athens. Evidently, he
had seen nothing in his extensive experience of the church to make him
qualify this statement, or even argue for it. If the baptism of infants had
been introduced only in recent years, or was only practised in one area
of the church known to him, it seems highly unlikely that Origen could
have made such a sweeping claim for it. Origen possessed one of the
most acute and questioning minds of the early church. If he could say,
as an established point of reference which did not need the support of
argument, that infant baptism was a practice received from the apostles,
then at the very least we must conclude that infant baptism was so
thoroughly established and so widespread by the early third century that
belief in its apostolic origin could pass without question.

  Aland (1963 48) discounted the argument that Origen could not have
written in this way about infant baptism if he had come across contrary
evidence on his travels. Aland argued that to claim this (as Jeremias 1960
70 had done) ignores the mentality and methods of Church Fathers
engaged in controversy, quite apart from the consideration that there is
nothing in the text to indicate it. According to Aland, Origen's defence
of infant baptism merely shows that there were people who questioned
it. Certainly, there *were* people who questioned the appropriateness of
infant baptism, but the point is that their appeal was to *principle*, while
Origen's was to *practice*. When the argument is seen in that light, it is
not hard to distinguish the conservatives championing the *status quo*
from the radicals with plans to reform it.

  We might expect that if the baptism of infants was introduced by the
late second-century church, the theology of the church's leadership
would of necessity have been favourable to it, otherwise, how could it
have gained a foothold? So it is significant that Origen was just as
theologically troubled by infant baptism as Tertullian, though for
different reasons. In his *Homilies on Luke* (*Homily* 14.49), Origen dealt
with a question which was apparently a live issue for his circle, one which
'the brethren often ask', namely, 'Why should children be baptized for
the remission of sins, or at what point had they sinned?' Origen's answer
to those who were puzzled by this was that they were being cleansed
from the 'uncleanness' (he cannot bring himself to say 'sin') which
attaches to everyone who is born. Infant baptism ran counter to the
prevailing assumption of the 'innocence' of children which we have

already seen expressed by Tertullian. Origen seemed to be struggling to convince his readers (and perhaps himself) that this rite was as well-founded theologically as it was historically. He gives the strong impression that, if infant baptism had not already existed, and if it had not a strong weight of tradition behind it, neither he nor his contemporaries would have invented it.

Our final third-century witness is Cyprian, Bishop of Carthage (d.258). Cyprian touched on infant baptism in response to an enquiry from a fellow bishop, Fidus, who, like Tertullian in the previous generation (Cyprian, *Letter* 64) had difficulties with the practice of infant baptism. But Fidus's problems were different. He proposed that baptism should be administered on the eighth day, as was circumcision. Another difficulty, which perhaps explains his reluctance to baptize on the second or third day after birth, centred on the kiss of peace which was given at baptism. There was, he suggested, something disgusting about small babies – they 'still bear traces of uncleanness', as Fidus seems to have put it. Could one expect a bishop to come into such intimate contact with them? Cyprian, having consulted the bishops of North Africa, answered Fidus quite directly by reminding him that in kissing the baby, he was kissing the hand of God, which had so recently finished this new creation. He ruled that children need the grace of baptism as soon as possible, and therefore should be baptized two or three days after birth.

We may wonder whether Fidus's wish to delay baptism, as well as being based on an explicit appeal to the Old Testament, was also echoing the customary *dies lustricus*, the day of purifying sacrifice, which, as we saw in chapter one (p.3.21), took place on the eighth day of a Roman girl's life; the ninth of a boy's. Cyprian seems to be championing a distinctly Christian attitude to the newborn. Christian baptism, unlike either circumcision in the Jewish community or the Roman *dies lustricus*, did not wait until the child had proved its viability at the end of the first perilous week of life. Acceptance in baptism was virtually immediate and not depedent on survival; the newborn child, Cyprian insisted, was to be treated as a person from the start of life.

But whatever their differences on matters of detail, both Cyprian and Fidus clearly accepted infant baptism as a normal part of the church's life.

We can now return to the question we asked earlier about Tertullian – whether, in questioning the practice of baptizing infants, he was a conservative or an innovator. Our third-century witnesses seem to suggest that infant baptism was a widespread and well-established custom. Origen traced it back to the apostles, and did not expect anyone to contradict him. Indeed, none of our sources, including Tertullian, does contradict Origen's claim. Tertullian could be overwhelmingly crushing with those who had introduced innovations of which he disapproved (and remarkably indulgent towards practices of which he approved, even when their apostolic origin was doubtful, see *On the Soldier's Crown* 3f.: *NE* 171f.). It would have been his best argument simply to say that the baptism of infants was a novelty brought into the church one or two generations previously. The fact that he *did* not use such an argument suggests strongly that he *could* not.

Those who, like Tertullian or Fidus, were beginning to ask whether the custom was justified or to demand that the practice should be altered, appear to be the innovators. They could not play the strongest card of all: the claim to apostolic authority. They could only, with Tertullian, point to the danger of post-baptismal sin, or with Fidus, appeal to their own dignity in performing the rite.

The case argued here, that infant baptism was a well-established custom by the beginning of the third century, is not held by all who have investigated the subject. One major argument against it is the fact that baptismal rites, from the very earliest days, envisage adult and not child candidates. Hippolytus, for instance, our first witness to what happened at baptismal ceremonies, was clearly describing a rite appropriate for adults, not children (*Apostolic Tradition* 21f.: *NE* 141–3). Interrogation of candidates, public declaration of faith and exorcism were all part of early ceremonies of baptism, and candidates were always treated as if they were able to exercise faith for themselves. Parents or sponsors might speak for them, but otherwise no concessions were made to the possibility that candidates might be children; still less, newborn infants. From this observation it is argued that originally all baptisms were adult baptisms, but that pressure to baptize infants grew up in the late second century. This pressure probably came from parents anxious about their children, but the form of baptism had already become fixed, and children were baptized using a rite which originated in the period before children were ever considered as candidates for baptism. If children were baptized from the start, the question runs, why did the early church not develop a rite appropriate to them?

This argument is not as strong as it sounds. For one thing, one might ask the question of the third-century church just as easily as of the first- or second-century church. The third century was quite liturgically innovative in other directions, so why should the church in that period not have made alterations to its developing liturgy to cope with the supposed new situation of infant candidates? But the real answer lies elsewhere. It is to be found in the observations we have already made on the way the early church treated children. Children were present at worship from the earliest times, as we have seen, yet Christian liturgy made no concessions to their presence. In view of the fact that the ancient world did not share our developmental view of human growth, it would be surprising if the early Christians had produced specialized liturgy of any sort for children. So it is not surprising that they should not have developed a baptismal liturgy for children.

Given the strong emphasis on the household as the sphere of instruction of the young in the faith (see pp.73-9, above), it is natural to suppose that infants being baptized would be regarded as the full responsibility of their parents. It is anachronistic to expect the early church to have treated infants as individuals or children as developing personalities for whom specially tailored material had to be produced.

It is no doubt true that baptismal ceremonies were modelled around the preparation of an adult convert. In the very earliest years of the church, only adult converts and their households were received into the community. But the church saw no reason to alter its rites as children were born in the community and were brought to baptism. To us, such ceremonies seem inappropriate to infants or children, but the third-century church did not perceive a difficulty in adminstering these ceremonies in the case of children, and we have no reason to suppose that the second-, or even the first-century church would have seen a problem here, either.

We should also add that the supposed pressure from parents to have their children baptized, is entirely hypothetical. We have no evidence of pressure *to* baptize infants. The pressure about which our sources inform us was exerted entirely in the opposite direction: to *stop* baptizing infants (Tertullian, and the 'brethren' who questioned Origen).

Augustine's Doctrine of Infant Baptism

We have argued that those who, like Tertullian, started to question the received practice of baptizing infants, were innovators in the third century. But the innovators had some measure of success. We find evidence in the third and fourth centuries of Christian parents not bringing children for baptism until they reached a fairly mature age. Several Christian funerary inscriptions from this period tell of children who evidently had not been baptized until their fatal illness, and then received baptism on their deathbeds, the so-called 'clinical baptism'. The first literary reference we have to clinical baptism is the baptism of Novatian (c.240 AD), who fell seriously ill while undergoing exorcism as an adult convert prior to receiving baptism. He seemed unlikely to live, and so was hurriedly baptized by mere sprinkling, rather than immersion, and without the normal accompanying rituals (Eusebius, *Ecclesiastical History*, 6.43.13). Novatian, incidentally, survived and went on to be a troublesome schismatic. But this hurried and emergency form of baptism was used also in the case of children who had not been baptized as infants and whose illness called for urgent action.

We have, amongst others, the examples of Apronianus, baptized just before he died at the age of one year, nine months and six days; Tyche, baptized on the day of her death aged one year ten months fifteen days; Irene, baptized a week before she died at eleven months and six days; and Marcianus, aged twelve, baptized a day before he died (Jeremias 1960 42, 78–80; Aland 1963 76–9). These are apparently third-century inscriptions (the Marcianus inscription has the date 268), and are from Rome.

Jeremias took the inscriptions which he discussed as evidence for infant baptism in the third century. Aland argued the contrary from the same material. He noted that when we have inscriptions giving unambiguous reference to baptism, and recording the child's age at baptism (as in the examples above), they are older children and not infants, strictly speaking. Since the children had not previously been baptized in infancy, the inscriptions are evidence against the practice of infant baptism in the third and fourth centuries. Aland dismissed Jeremias' suggestion that these inscriptions giving the date of baptism were commissioned by pagan families, who accepted Christian baptism for their children *in extremis*. He pointed out that Christian artistic motifs and phrases on the Marcianus inscription could only have come from a Christian family (Aland 1963 78f.).

It would seem that in the third century neither the church's theologians nor its lay members really knew what to think or do about the baptism of infants. The most likely explanation of the funerary inscriptions is that we see in them the result in ordinary Christians' lives of the argument which Tertullian was putting forward. He did not deny that infants or children could be baptized. He simply questioned whether it was wise to commit children to the demanding life of the baptized Christian. In *On Baptism* Tertullian implies that children could and should be baptized when it is urgently necessary (i.e. when seriously ill). But why should sponsors imperil themselves, he asked, 'if it is not so very necessary' (*si non tam necesse est*)? When the forgiveness of sin after baptism was such a serious matter, it was the wisest course to defer baptism until as late as possible. The funerary inscriptions reveal a Christian community in which (unlike most modern churches practising believers' baptism) children may be baptized. That is why they were baptized before their death. But it was a community in which post-baptismal sin was treated with such seriousness (unlike most churches which today baptize infants) that no child who was expected to live would be committed to the arduous path of the baptized Christian. Hence these children were not baptized before their final illnesses.

This success of the Tertullianist argument is also seen in the biographies of several prominent leaders of the fourth-century church. Gregory of Nazianzus (b.328/30, the first child of Christian parents known *not* to have been baptized as a child), Basil the Great, John Chrysostom and Augustine, though all born to at least one Christian parent, and all advocating infant (or at least child) baptism in their teaching, were all themselves baptized only in adult life. The church into which they were born and in which they grew up was one in which infant baptism was permissible, but not required. Augustine's mother, Monica, could have had the infant Augustine baptized, but preferred to delay, because, Augustine explained, she was afraid of the heavy guilt of post-baptismal sin (Augustine, *Confessions* 1.17). She came close to giving in when Augustine was seriously ill as a child, but held out, because, as Augustine later expressed it: 'My mother well knew how many great tides of temptation threatened me before I grew up, and she chose to let them beat upon the as yet unmoulded clay rather than upon the finished image which had received the stamp of baptism'.

Christian parents in the fourth century had the choice of allowing their children to be baptized, as the old custom had been, or leaving them till a later and more settled stage of their lives, as religious prudence seemed to dictate. Monica chose to leave her son unbaptized, and no doubt this was the choice of many devout parents at the time. But a change was taking place in the time of Augustine, to which his own powerful theological mind would give a strong impetus. Significantly, Augustine noted that 'even nowadays' (*etiam nunc*) one could hear people say of a child, 'Leave him alone and let him do it. He is not yet baptized' (*Confessions* 1.18). The phrase 'even nowadays' suggests that a change of attitude was under way. Augustine himself, though loath to criticize the mother he revered, questioned the wisdom of her decision, and wished that he had been baptized in infancy. He belonged to a different generation, among whom the habit of delaying baptism was no longer the norm.

Augustine's own contribution was to give a theological rationale for infant baptism for the first time in the church's history. Augustine articulated a belief in original sin, that is, a conviction that each human being is born, not only with an inborn tendency to turn away from God (which all Christian thinkers had agreed was the case), but also already guilty of sin. He derived this conviction from such biblical texts as Psalm 51:5, 'I was brought forth in iniquity, and in sin did my mother conceive me', and Romans 5:12, which Augustine wrongly understood to mean 'through one man sin entered into the world, and through sin death, and so death passed on into all men, in whom [i.e.Adam] all sinned' (*Against Two Pelagian Epistles*, 4.7). Augustine maintained that the guilt of Adam's sin is passed on to the newborn infant, and that each person, from birth, is part of a humanity which he could describe as 'a lump of sin' (*To Simplicianus* 1.2.16).

In Augustine, infant baptism found what it had so far lacked: a theological champion. His view of original sin gave the church a reason for the practice of baptizing newborn babies: baptism confers the forgiveness of sins, but what sins could the newborn baby be guilty of if not original or birth-sin (*Nupt. & Concup.* 1.22)? We have to realize also that the baptismal rite known to Augustine included elaborate rituals connected with exorcism, such as 'exsufflation', or breathing on the face of the baptismal candidate, to represent the coming of the Holy Spirit and the banishment of all evil spirits. Augustine could appeal to this practice to ask why these rituals should be necessary, if the child is not initially under the power of Satan (*Unfinished Work against Julian* 3.199).

Historically, the answer to Augustine's question is that the baptismal rite had been developed with adult converts in view, and was never adapted to children, as we have seen. But Augustine's case carried the day. His main opponents in his baptismal controversies, the Pelagians, did not deny the validity of infant baptism, but attributed a positive value to it (admission as a member of Christ), and denied that in the case of children baptism conferred the remission of sins, because they believed that children had no sins to be remitted. To Augustine, their view suggested that there were two baptisms, one (for infants) which did not confer the remission of sins, and another (for adults) which did. This, he maintained, was in defiance of the credal statement: 'I believe in one baptism'.

Augustine was the great theologian of grace. His strong emphasis on the grace of God given in baptism permitted, in less able defenders of his position, a mechanistic view of grace, as if it were an object which could be given by appropriately-ordained persons to appropriate candidates. But his stress on the grace of God enabled the church to overcome its fear of post-baptismal sin. If that fear had continued to run its course through the church, the typical pattern of initiation might eventually have been that of the Emperor Constantine, who was baptized only on his deathbed.

From the time of Augustine until the Reformation, the baptism of infants was firmly established, not only as the practice of the church, but also as a rite built on solid theological foundations. But Augustine's achievement was destined in time to be called into question. The Anabaptists questioned the validity of those foundations by pointing out the absence of explicit cases of infant baptism in the Scriptures, and by asking whether the doctrine of baptism in the New Testament could really encompass infants. The developing Baptist tradition further undermined these foundations by raising with new urgency the issues behind Tertullian's questions. How can grace be ministered to someone who is not conscious of faith? The Evangelical movement from the eighteenth century onwards found infant baptism fitted uneasily with its emphasis on personal faith as the means of grace in the believer's life. In consequence, 'believers' baptism' became the norm in several denominations which arose from that movement or were influenced by it. And finally, Augustine's case, which rested on a particular understanding of inborn guilt inherited biologically from Adam, would have difficulty surviving in a world in which the Genesis story was no longer read literally.

At the very least, Augustine's rationale for infant baptism is today in need of re-interpretation. More radically, it could be argued that his whole position has crumbled, and has left the practice of infant baptism once again as a rite in search of a theology. So it is that the historical question which we posed earlier, namely whether the early church baptized infants, brings us round to a theological question, namely whether the baptism of infants or children fits the purpose and nature of baptism in the New Testament.

Baptism in the New Testament

In the third century, infant baptism was already a strongly-established practice but it was coming under critical scrutiny from those who were worried about post-baptismal sin. No participant in the third-century debate about infant baptism claimed that the baptism of young children was an innovation which had crept in since the time of the apostles. Even those who thought it unwise to baptize infants accepted that infant baptism was what Origen claimed it to be: a custom deriving from the apostles.

We have to ask whether they were right. In which direction does the New Testament evidence itself point, both as to practice and as to the theology of baptism?

Household baptisms

When we look at the New Testament practice, we have no record of a child being baptized, but we do have the record of whole households being baptized at the same time (the household of Lydia in Acts 16:15 and the Philippian gaoler in Acts 16:33; of Stephanas in 1 Cor.1:16). Again we run into the problem of 'not counting the children'. It was not of any consequence to Luke or Paul to tell their readers whether these households had any children, and if so, whether they were included or excluded when the other members were baptized.

The conversion of Crispus in Corinth with 'all his household' is narrated in Acts 18:8, and in 1 Corinthians 1:14 Paul says that he baptized Crispus but says nothing about his household. It could be argued that this was typical of 'household baptisms'; that the head of the household was converted and baptized, but the children would have to wait until they had reached the age of discretion to be baptized. There are many imponderables here. It is possible that only Crispus was baptized. But it is equally possible that only Crispus was baptized by Paul, while other members of the household were baptized by Paul's companions.

There is certainly a wholesale aspect to these household baptisms. No New Testament source gives us any indication of how distinctions were made within households at conversion, if they were made. If the husband was converted, was the wife baptized? If some children were allowed to respond to the preaching, while younger ones were judged too young, what were their ages? What about older children who expressed a contrary opinion? The New Testament gives no guidance on such important questions, and indeed no indication that the issues were even raised. The simplest solution is that the household which was baptized when its head was converted was just that: the whole household, including wife and children. Slaves were probably differently treated. We know from the New Testament that there were Christian slaves in pagan households (1 Tim.6:1f.) and, from Aristides in the second century, we find that Christian masters had pagan slaves, whom they would seek to persuade to accept the faith, but could not or would not compel to conform (Aristides, *Apology* 15.6, see above, pp.85f.).

This simple solution to the enigma of the household baptisms still falls short of proof. It is quite possible to read the evidence of the household baptisms either way. If one is persuaded on other grounds that the New Testament church baptized infants, one can readily imagine that all children in these households, infants included, were included in baptism. But if one is persuaded that the New Testament church could not have offered baptism to children too young to make a conscious response to the gospel for themselves, then one can equally readily suppose that these household baptisms deliberately excluded children below a certain age.

Baptism and faith

If the practice of the apostolic period, as the New Testament records it, is inconclusive, what about the principle or the theology of baptism in the New Testament? What guidance do we have there?

Since the Reformation a key text has been Mark 16:16: 'Those who believe the gospel and receive baptism will be saved'. It neatly summarizes the theological case against the baptism of infants. Baptism is the sign and seal of the believer's profession of faith. It must therefore be reserved for those who have professed faith after hearing and receiving the gospel. Any administration of water in other circumstances cannot really be called 'baptism' at all, because it fails to respect the order, hearing-believing-baptism. Baptism in the New Testament called for repentance and for faith, and so could not have been administered to infants incapable of exercising either.

Unfortunately for the neatness of this case, most scholars today would reject the longer ending of Mark, from which Mark 16:16 comes, as inauthentic, though, even as a product of the second-century church, it can stand as a summary of how the New Testament presents baptism. Adults in the narrative of Acts are indeed summoned to repentance and faith before coming to the waters of baptism. The letters of the New

Testament speak of baptism in terms which presuppose a conscious and adult exercise of faith (e.g. Rom.6:3ff., 1 Cor.12:13, Gal.3:27, 1 Pet.3:21). If the New Testament speaks in this way about baptism, can there be any room for infant baptism in the New Testament? Is not the practice of infant baptism excluded by the theology of baptism in the New Testament? So the Baptist tradition, as it has developed since the Reformation, has argued and continues to argue.

Such a reading of the New Testament has the great strength of being supported by the New Testament's silence about any baptism of infants. It has the great merit of working from the clear beliefs of the New Testament writers about baptism and reconstructing a picture of New Testament practice from observing those beliefs. But the case is not entirely closed even when these things have been said.

To us it may seem logical to say that, if a candidate for baptism is expected to demonstrate a response of faith to the gospel, a child cannot make that response, and that therefore a child is not a suitable candidate for baptism. But in the early church nobody seems to have followed such logic. Tertullian's worry was, as has been seen, the seriousness of sin after baptism, not the infant's lack of capacity for faith. The first person to suggest that baptism be delayed until a child has developed some capacity for understanding was Gregory of Nazianzus (c.325–390), and he recommended the age of three because he thought children could then answer the baptismal questions with some grasp of what they meant (*Oratio* 40, *In Sanctum Baptisma* 28). Even in that instance, the concern was not directly with the child's inability to exercise faith.

If children of Christian parents were not baptized until reaching years of discretion, we might expect to find some hint in early Christian literature of discussion about what is the appropriate age for their profession of faith to be accepted. But in the first two centuries of the church we do not have any instances of children who had grown up within the church being baptized in later life. This did not happen until the third century, when it was fear, not faith, which was the issue; fear of post-baptismal sin which led to people delaying baptism until well into adulthood – and in some cases until their death-beds. Apart from these delayed baptisms, we know of only two sorts of baptismal candidates: converts and infants. Grown children of Christian parents, who had waited until they could make a valid profession of faith, do not appear.

The answer to this seems to lie in the household which has been observed as the basic building block of the church from its earliest days. Even in the gospels, we recall that the ministry of Jesus was always through the parents. The instruction and care of the young was a major responsibility of the household from the start of the church's life. Children were perceived as embedded in the family. It was natural that parents should answer for them in all things pertaining to relations with the world beyond the family. It would have been natural, too, that at conversion parents would expect their children to be baptized along with themselves. The perception of the child as an autonomous individual, free to make up its own mind in due course, is a modern one, alien to the world of the New Testament. We should not project it onto the New Testament and its writers.

The institution of circumcision may have prepared the way for the baptism of infants in the Christian church. The circumcision of the male Jewish child is certainly a good example of the embedding of the child in the family. We have seen how Bishop Fidus in the third century made the identification between the old form of initiation and the new (Cyprian, *Letter* 64). The New Testament gives us no explicit reason to suppose that baptism took the place of circumcision for the children of the Christian community. Some writers on the subject seem to have supposed that, having rejected circumcision, Christians had solved the problem of the initiation of children into the community, as though Gentiles had no rituals of their own concerning children. But in chapter one we saw that Roman society had the *dies lustricus*, and no doubt other cultures had their own rites, too. If baptism did not replace circumcision and the *dies lustricus*, what did take their place?

Not to accept the baptism of infants in the New Testament, is to suppose that the first Christians had no rite of initiation for children. We have to recognize how odd that would be for people whose lives were filled with ritual. As we saw in the first chapter, both Gentile and Jewish communities had important rituals surrounding the birth and acceptance of children into the community. We know that the Christians abandoned circumcision at an early stage: in Acts 21:21, the Jerusalem elders say to Paul that they have heard that a major part of Paul's 'apostasy' was to teach that children should not be circumcised. But, when both Jews and Gentiles were used to marking the birth of children with important ceremonies, are we to suppose that when they became Christians they decided to forego all ceremony and rite? It is difficult for us to put ourselves in the position of people whose lives were marked by rites at every stage. For the first Christians to have had *no* ritual to mark a child's entry into the community would have made them a very eccentric group in their world. Baptism is the only Christian rite of entry known to us. If the first Christians did not baptize their infants, just how did they mark their birth?

One could argue that the first Christians were eccentric in precisely this way, that they were indeed content to abandon all rites of initiation for their children, and that only the pressure to conform to a very ritualized society made them adopt infant baptism at a later date. So, in the mid-second century Aristides could say of the Christians: 'When a child is born to any one of them, they praise God' (*Apology* 15.11: *NE* 54). This could be evidence for a thanksgiving ceremony at the birth of a child. But Aristides was not giving an account of Christian worship, he was arguing for the harmlessness of Christians and the naturalness of their way of life. It is equally possible that Christians did what would seem most obvious and adopted their ceremony of initiation also for the children born to them.

The most that can be said on this point is that the existence of circumcision and its pagan parallels *may* have led the first Christians to expect some form of initiation into the community to correspond with the place of circumcision under the old covenant.

We have seen how Ephesians and Colossians address children in the course of their ethical instruction (Eph.6:1–3, Col.3:20). We must assume that children were part of the congregation; they would have heard the whole of those letters read. Both letters have much to say which implies that the recipients were baptized (Eph.2:5; 4:5; 4:20–4, Col.2:6; 2:20–3:4). There is no hint here that the congregation contained adults who had been baptized, and to whom these things applied, and children who were unbaptized, and to whom they did not. It seems a more natural understanding that the congregation contained both adults, who had received Christ in adulthood and had been baptized on profession of faith, and children, who had been baptized as infants and who were 'growing up into Christ' (Eph.4:15). This would have been the typical Christian congregation of the first century. Those who entered the community from outside, entered by the gateway of baptism. Those who entered from within, born within the community, entered by the same gateway, for, as Ephesians says, 'there is one Lord, one faith, one baptism' (Eph.4:5).

Conclusion

There is every reason to suppose that Origen was right in thinking that the baptism of children of believing parents began in the apostolic era.

This would explain his testimony that it had begun then, and Tertullian's inability to claim that it had not.

The baptism of children is entirely what we would expect, given the attitude of the early Christian community to their children as those included in the worshipping life of the church as part of their families. The silence of the early writers on this issue is also what we would expect, given their attitude to children, who were the focus of a great deal of thought or reflection.

Our conclusion (and necessarily a tentative one) is that the first Christians baptized children from the time of the church's origins. Children were included in the 'household baptisms' which the New Testament records in its stories of conversions. Subsequently, within the household-based churches of the early Christians, children were baptized as they were born. All this took place in the first and second centuries without a great deal of reflection. However, in the early third century the church began to acquire its first theologians; men who attempted to weave together Christian belief into a harmonious whole. This generation of thinkers soon noticed that the church's established practice of baptizing infants, although so far unquestioned, sat rather uneasily alongside both the widespread assumption of children's 'innocence' (i.e. guiltlessness before God), and the growing concern about sins after baptism, whose remission could by no means be taken for granted. Consistency demanded either that the practice be changed (Tertullian) or that the beliefs be modified (Origen).

In the third century we find two different understandings of baptism at large in the church as a result of this uncertainty. On the one hand there were conservatives, such as Cyprian, who continued to uphold the propriety of baptism administered almost immediately after birth. On the other hand were those people persuaded to delay baptism by a new understanding of the rite as a culmination, rather than a starting-point, of the Christian life. Parents seem not to have been troubled by the thought of what would happen to their children if they died unbaptized. Quite the contrary, they seem to have been troubled by the thought of what would happen to their children if they were baptized and lived. If they baptized their children, how would these children then find forgiveness if they sinned, as they were almost bound to do? And after all, baptism could be administered swiftly in the case of serious illness, and was so administered, if we may believe the funerary inscriptions.

Christian theology developed, as much as anything, by Christians looking at what the church *did*, such as calling Jesus 'Lord', and working out what these things *meant* in theological terms, for instance in its doctrine of Christ. So, in the case of baptism, the qualms expressed by Tertullian and Origen, the delay in baptism witnessed by the inscriptions, the questionings of Bishop Fidus, all these features were part of the process by which the church worked out what baptism meant. Those who believe, as Aland did, that the baptism of infants was a late development, ascribe the uncertainties of the third and fourth centuries to the introduction of the novel practice of infant baptism into a church which had not known it previously. But no one suggested at the time that the practice was novel; the only new feature after Tertullian was the amount of reflection and thought devoted to baptism. It was only in the thought of Augustine that the church found a theology to match and explain its ancient practice of baptizing infants. As with the development of Christology, the growth of a theology of baptism threw out some branches which were destined not to bear fruit. But the mature theology of baptism which we find in Augustine was not the imposition of something alien: it was the outgrowth of what had been implicit since the time of the New Testament.

No interpretation of the evidence will amount to proof of the case for or against infant baptism as a practice of the New Testament church, unless some startling new piece of the puzzle should come to light. The interpretation which is given here is offered as the most convincing way of making sense of those pieces of the puzzle which are at present to hand.

Children and the Eucharist

Our understanding of children at Communion is similar to the picture we may draw of children and baptism. We have to proceed by way of inference from a few stray references, because the issue is not dealt with directly by any writer before Augustine in the late fourth and early fifth century. But from the fragmentary evidence we have, it appears that the participation of children in Communion was a normal and unproblematic aspect of Christian worship in the first four centuries.

Since the relation of children to the Eucharist is not such a well-known or thoroughly-discussed topic as infant baptism, it may be instructive to take the story beyond the New Testament and early church, and make a brief survey of the way in which children have been admitted to the Eucharist or excluded from it over the course of the centuries.

The New Testament tells us nothing directly about whether children received the Eucharist or not. We have seen that children were present at worship, including (we presume) the Eucharist. There was a theological assumption that children of at least one Christian parent were in the community of faith, that they were 'holy' (1 Cor.7:14). If the earliest Christians saw some similarities between the Eucharist which commemorated the sacrifice of Christ, whom Paul described as 'our Passover lamb' (1 Cor.5:7), and the Passover celebration already familiar to them, then we might expect that children would partake of the Christian meal as they had done of the Jewish one (Exod.12:21-7). But this expectation is little more than a guess, and all the witness of the New Testament falls far short of solid evidence one way or the other.

All we can say is that there was no reason for children not to receive the Eucharist in the time of the New Testament, especially if we are right in our argument that children of Christian parents were baptized from the earliest years of the church, and there are several indications that it would have been appropriate for them to do so. We can also say that when we begin to have some firm evidence, in the third century, we find children receiving Communion without the matter being controversial. If a change had occurred in the century and a half which separates the New Testament from our first reference to child Communion, then it was a change which had happened without causing a stir. It would also have been a change in a period when children generally were being relegated to a sphere of family religion and away from full participation in the church. If children were first admitted to Communion during the second century, it would have been a move very much against the tide of the times. It seems, on balance, more probable that they were admitted to the Lord's Table from the start.

Our first witness to child Communion is Cyprian of Carthage (d.258). In a passage from his book *On the Lapsed*, which we have already referred to (p.71), we find that he gives a significant glimpse into the practice of the African church in the early third century. He tells the story of a child, whose nurse had taken her to a pagan ritual without the parents' knowledge. There, the child had been given some of the sacrificial food to eat. When the little girl was returned to her mother, her Christian parents knew nothing about it until her mother took her to Christian worship. At worship, the first sign of trouble was the child's obvious disturbance in the course of the service. When she was offered the Communion cup she at first refused, but the deacon who was administering it persisted. However, when she took the wine she immediately vomited (*On the Lapsed*, 25). It is interesting that Cyprian says the girl was not able to speak or reveal to her parents what had gone on at the pagan sacrifice. He was apparently thinking of a child before the age of speech, and he thought it was quite normal for a child of that age to receive Communion.

Elsewhere in the same work, Cyprian reviews the fate of those who compromised under persecution by taking part in pagan sacrifices. Children were involved, and he says that, though innocent, they have had their spiritual nourishment polluted:

> Infants also, in the arms of their parents, either carried or led, lost, while yet little ones, what in the very beginning of their nativity they had gained. Will not they, when the day of judgement comes, say: 'We have done nothing: nor have we forsaken the Lord's bread and cup to hasten freely to a profane contract.' (Cyprian, *On the Lapsed* 9)

It is interesting to see that these children had been accustomed to receiving Communion from birth ('the very beginning of their nativity').

The *Apostolic Constitutions* (8.13), a work dealing with church order from fourth century Syria, refer to the custom of the Syrian church in admitting children to Communion. It stipulates the order in which the church is to receive Communion: first bishops, then presbyters, deacons, subdeacons, readers, singers and ascetics; after that come their equivalents among the women, deaconesses, virgins and widows; then the children are to come and receive before the rest of the congregation. This provision for the children to receive Communion before the main body of adults is rather similar to the provision in the *Apostolic Tradition* of Hippolytus that children are to receive baptism before the adults.

We have a touching and personal testimony to the practice of child Communion in a funeral inscription from Catania in Sicily, dated to the early fourth century (Diehl, *ILCV* 1.1549). The inscription commemorates a little girl, Julia Florentina, who was taken seriously ill at around eighteen months of age. Her parents hurriedly requested baptism, which was administered. She was then given Communion before her death. Julia Florentina's moving epitaph does not refer to a regular reception of Communion in the normal worship of the church, as Cyprian and the Apostolic Constitutions do, but it shows us that small children were allowed to receive Communion immediately after their baptism.

These early witnesses merely record, in passing, the practice of the church of their day. They describe the practice without explaining what was happening or justifying it. Augustine, at the turn of the fourth and fifth centuries, was the first to make this inherited practice a matter of reflection. One scriptural passage in particular seems to have moulded Augustine's thought on this topic: John 6:53 'Unless you eat the flesh of the Son of Man and drink his blood you can have no life in you'. Augustine took the force of this to be that there could be no halfway house between the unbaptized and the communicant; if children were baptized, then they should have the life of Christ in them, but how could they have his life without eating the flesh of the Son of Man and drinking his blood? This was Augustine's basic point of reference in discussing this issue, as he did on several occasions (*On the Merits of Sinners* 1.20; *Sermon* 8; *Letter* 106). From this axiom, Augustine built a powerful case for the admission of children to Communion. Indeed, his contemporary, Pope Innocent I, used the argument in the opposite direction: the necessity for children to receive Communion proved the necessity for them to be baptized (*Letter* 182.93).

In the Eastern church, the admission of children to Communion continued to be normal, as it remains today. But things took a different course in the West. Despite the weighty support of Augustine, both custom and theology combined to squeeze child Communion out of the Western church.

This pressure on child Communion came partly from a doctrinal source: the development of a more realistic view of transubstantiation began to make theologians uneasy about child Communion. While John 6:53 had impressed itself upon Augustine as a guiding principle, the church of the high Middle Ages was more exercised by 1 Corinthians 11:27–9: 'Anyone who eats the bread or drinks the cup of the Lord unworthily will be guilty of offending against the body and blood of the Lord . . .' The Third Council of Tours (c.19) in the ninth century appealed to this text to dissuade priests from giving the elements indiscriminately to children.

Nonetheless, children were still admitted to Communion during the early Middle Ages, though their position set them slightly apart from adults, and led to certain particular provisions being made for them. The Second Council of Mâcon (Canon 6: 585 AD), stipulated that the remains of the consecrated bread, moistened with wine, should be given to children at the mass on Wednesdays and Fridays, and that these children, like the priest himself, should be fasting (Hefele & Leclerq 3 1909 209f.). Walter of Orleans, writing in the mid-ninth century, counselled that a priest should always have the sacrament reserved, so that he could

administer it immediately to anyone who was sick, or to an infant
('*parvulus*' – Walter seems to mean a small child), so that they should
not die without the comfort of the sacrament (Capitula 7, *Patrologia
Latina* 119.734f.). Pope Paschal II (Pope 1099–1118) laid down that
young children, as a concession to their inability to digest bread and wine
separately, should have their communion bread dipped into the wine. The
same rule applied to the sick (*Letter* 535 *Patrologia Latina* 163.442).

The restriction on the communion of children becomes clear in the
twelfth and thirteenth centuries. A few generations after Pope Paschal's
ruling, we find Bishop Odo of Paris advising, in 1175, that children were
not to be given consecrated bread. By way of compensation children were
allowed to drink the wine rinsed out of the chalice at the ablutions
(*Patrologia Latina* 212.66f.).

The growing reverence for the elements of the Eucharist finally
debarred children from Communion. The logic of this view was pressed
to its conclusion at the Fourth Lateran Council (1215), which linked the
duty of taking Communion with the child's arrival at years of discretion
(DS812). The Council decreed that a child should not receive it before
he or she was able to distinguish the host from ordinary food, a stage
originally set at around seven years of age but later pushed back to ten
to fourteen years. This was the first time that a specific age limit was set
on receiving Communion. This restriction on children's Communion
happened at a time in the church's life when most lay people received
Communion infrequently, if at all. The Fourth Lateran Council, as well
as introducing an age limit for reception, laid down that lay people should
receive the sacrament at least once a year (cap.21). This minimum
requirement seems to have become the normal maximum for the majority
of worshippers. The reverence for the sacrament in the later Middle Ages
was such that reception had become virtually a privilege of the
priesthood.

The Catholic Reformation of the sixteenth century reinforced the
ruling of the Lateran Council on child Communion: the Council of Trent
explicitly anathematized anyone who said that children below the age of
discretion could receive Communion (Section 21, Canon 4: DS1734).
Protestant apologists were able to make play with the discrepancy
between the pronouncement of the Council of Trent, the official
definition of Catholic doctrine, and the clear statements of Augustine,
one of the leading Church Fathers. But Roman Catholic practice in the
twentieth century has reverted to something more like the church's
primitive practice, permitting children to receive Communion at a much

younger age than has been normal in, say, the Anglican Church. It has become the custom in many places for children to receive their first Communion before confirmation, at around the age of seven. The age of 'about the seventh year' for first Communion was stipulated by Pope Pius X in the decree 'Quam Singulari' (8th August 1910).

Among the churches of the Reformation much of the theology of the Fourth Lateran Council was called into question. But on the matter of children and Communion, there was a remarkable degree of continuity throughout the diverging branches of the now divided church. The churches of the Reformation held on to the position established by the Lateran Council, even when they repudiated the Eucharistic theology with which the Council was associated.

The first movement towards restoring infant Communion in fact occurred before the Protestant Reformation, among the members of the Bohemian Utraquist movement of the fifteenth century. This movement of reform and spiritual renewal, as well as demanding that lay people should be allowed the wine at Communion and not merely bread only, made the Eucharist available to baptized infants. This became a central tenet of the Hussite Church which developed from the Utraquist movement. A strong sense of solidarity bonded the Hussites together, and their firm conviction was that the poor, the weak and the children should not be excluded from the community's central act of worship (Holeton 1981 9-15).

Theologians continued to read the Church Fathers, and were made aware of the testimonies to infant Communion which their writings contained. Proposals to revive the church's primitive practice were made sporadically. For instance, in the mid seventeenth century, the Anglican Bishop Bedel argued for a return to the primitive custom of including baptized children in the Eucharist. His appeal fell on deaf ears, though the learned Joseph Bingham in the early eighteenth century did the Bishop the courtesy of discussing his suggestion. Bingham rejected it, mainly on the grounds of an infant's inability to understand the sacrament, which made him or her unable to fulfil Jesus's command to 'do this in remembrance of me' (Bingham, 1855 5.378f.). The seventeenth-century debate in England and Wales is surveyed by Holeton (1981 16–21).

Within the Anglican church the pattern of growing up became settled: baptism in infancy, confirmation in adolescence, preceded by catechesis, and followed by admission to Communion. Other churches of the Reformation outside the Baptist tradition developed a corresponding pattern, with reception into membership taking the place of confirmation at years of discretion. This pattern left baptized children in precisely that anomalous position which had worried Augustine: supposedly incorporated in Christ by baptism, but denied access to the fellowship of the Lord's Table. The churches of the Baptist tradition had solved the difficulty by limiting both ordinances, baptism and Communion, to those who had reached years of discretion and who had given evidence of conscious faith. Those who retained infant baptism, but barred children from Communion, were in a less consistent position.

Eighteenth and nineteenth century reformers tried to do something for children, but paradoxically the rise of the Sunday School in the nineteenth century tended to confirm the place of the child as outside the church, preparing to come in (on the Sunday School's origins, see Laqueur 1976, and on its development, see Cliff 1986). In the twentieth century, new approaches to worship, particularly the Parish Communion, Children's Church and the Family Service, have brought children physically into the worship of the church (A study of an early experiment in this direction is Binfield 1994). A new recognition of childhood and its importance has made children a focus of concern and discussion. Coming together, these elements have raised afresh the question of how children fit theologically into the churches' life. Increasingly, churches which practise infant baptism are asking why, if children may be baptized, they should be refused Communion. And increasingly, they are coming to the conclusion that baptized children may indeed be admitted to the eucharistic fellowship of the church. So it is that contemporary problems and opportunities are bringing us back to reconsider the thought and practice of the first Christians.

Chapter 5

Contemporary Reflections

A future hisorian, wanting to study the place of children in our society, would be far better placed to carry out his work than we have been in our attempt to observe children in the New Testament and the early church. Children themselves, and childhood as a stage of life, have become the subjects of massive studies, which are proliferating all the time. Child development, both physiological and psychological, has been the centre of much attention, while thinking about education has also developed apace and produced a multitude of theories and accompanying practices. As a result, our knowledge of children and our understanding of childhood is much more articulate than in previous ages, including the time of the New Testament. Current theories about child development or education may be questioned and almost certainly will be superseded as time goes on, but these theories are built on systematic observation of children and analysis of evidence, not merely, as in the ancient world, on inherited custom and haphazard observations made by individuals.

In the Christian community, too, children have been given far more attention in the last century than in any previous period of the church's life. The week-by-week experience of worship in churches may not always reflect this growth of interest in children; in many churches children are still to be seen and not heard, and quite frequently they are not even to be seen. But the study of children and the Christian faith, at all levels from the abstract discussion of Christian initiation to the most practical details of child-rearing or preparation for all-age worship, has produced a large literature with issues and topics of its own. Children are on the churches' agenda in a way in which they have not been in previous ages.

The radically different situation in which we find ourselves today, when we compare the present day with the New Testament period, prompts two questions. Does the huge gap in culture between our time and theirs (which we explored in chapter one) mean that no texts from that era can really have anything to say today? And, if the New Testament and the early church (whose attitudes to children we looked at in chapters two to four) do indeed have something to say, how do we relate the first Christians' beliefs and practices to our present concerns?

The first question applies to all biblical interpretation. The reason for taking the trouble to look carefully at attitudes to children in the ancient world in chapter one was precisely to help us with the task of translating what the New Testament said and what the early church did into terms which make sense today. So, for example, when we take into consideration the disciplinary regime of the ancient household, we see that we have to take what is said about the punishment of children in Hebrews 12:7–11 as an observation of current practice, not as an injunction to beat children. This kind of translation of biblical material was already being made by some early Christians (see above, p.78).

The reason for trying to put the New Testament and early church material into a wider framework of interpretation in chapters two to four was to help us avoid taking texts in isolation, with the consequent danger of reading our understanding of children, childhood, family and church into our texts. We have to recognize that their world was different from ours, and we cannot take a complete blueprint for the church's treatment of children out of the pages of the New Testament. But in the New Testament we can find pointers or guidelines – and any church which calls itself Christian has to relate itself to the New Testament, in this as in other respects. The justification for attempting to uncover the place of children in the ministry of Jesus and in the life of the first churches is to make those foundational resources available to Christians today. If chapters one to four aimed to present the material in the original cultural 'language', this chapter is a brief essay in cultural translation: putting some of the things which were said *then* into terms which make sense *now*.

Answering the second question, about how we relate the sources we have examined to our concerns today, will be the task of the rest of this chapter. We shall consider these concerns in three contexts: concern for children, children and the church, and children and the family.

Christian Concern for Children

When we looked at children in the world of the New Testament, in the first chapter, we noted that a general concern for children, beyond the children of one's own immediate family, was hard to discover in the ancient world (pp.32-5). Even when Philo, the Jewish philosopher, paraded the evil of exposure of children, he saw it as a failure of parental responsibility, rather than something for which society at large was in any way responsible (p.4f).

The first Christians, with their household-based religion, did not immediately challenge or alter this perception. Their primary concern, too, was with the children of their own families (p.73-9). For the first Christians, children mainly featured in their thinking as one aspect of family life, not as a topic in and of themselves (pp.52, 58f).

But two things worked together to generalize and extend the scope of the Christians' concern for children. One was the respect for infant life which they drew from the ethical inheritance of Judaism. The other was the continuing presence in their tradition of the words of Jesus. They remembered that he had commended children as objects of care (Mk.9:37). So it is significant that in 374 AD, the Christian emperors Valentinian, Valens and Gratian made infanticide a crime punishable by death. Part of the consolidation of Christianity in the Roman Empire was to extend the protection of the law over the lives of young children.

In the history of Christianity there have been plenty of instances of failure to fulfil this general concern for the well-being of children. The abuse of children has been as widespread in so-called Christian societies as in others, and it would be naive to claim that the dominance of Christianity in Western culture has necessarily meant that children have been universally well cared for. But the example and words of Jesus have continued to have their effect, as have the frequent biblical injunctions to care for orphans. The foundation of orphanages has long been a traditional and characteristic feature of Christian philanthropy. In nineteenth century Britain, those who worked to promote legislation protecting children from exploitation in factories and mines were in many instances motivated by a Christian concern for infant life, derived from the teaching of Jesus. Lord Shaftesbury stands as a signal example. Equally, though, it would have to be said that many mill- and mine-owners were devout Christians, who could not see the application of the gospel words to their own child labour force. William Wilberforce, the tireless campaigner for the emancipation of slaves, is a case in point.

It is very easy to see the failings of other times and other people. But those who want to be disciples of Christ today have to work out the relevance of Jesus' words and actions for their own day and circumstances. If, in chapter two, we rightly discerned the meaning of Jesus's words and actions towards children, then there must be for

Christians a particular focus of concern for children; and not merely the children of their own household, nor just the children of the church community, but children simply as children, wherever they are and in whatever need they find themselves.

The Christian emperors in the fourth century, and the social reformers of the nineteenth, were trying to follow what they saw as the will of God for children, shown by Jesus. The challenge to discern God's will in specific action has not gone away. Indeed, in some respects the challenge has intensified, as improved communications bring desperate needs to our attention – not merely those on our own doorstep, but from around the world. Legislation may be important to protect those unable to protect themselves. Support of those agencies that work to care for children must be a major responsibility for Christians today, whether those agencies are specifically Christian or not.

Constant concern and practical care for children has to be an integral part of authentic Christian discipleship. And it is a task never finished. As soon as one scourge of children's lives is removed, whether it is infanticide in the Roman Empire, or child labour in Victorian Britain, another takes its place. Having removed child labour in Britain, we are aware of child exploitation in other parts of the world. Our increased openness about sexual matters makes us painfully aware of the sexual abuse of children, within the family and beyond. The Christian's commitment to this continuous task of vigilance in the care of children springs ultimately from obedience to the example of Christ himself.

Children in the Church

In much of Western society, churches today find themselves in circumstances nearer to those of the New Testament world than they have experienced for centuries. So, at one time, growing up to take one's place in the church community was simply one aspect of a child's general socialization. Today, churches are generally aware that there is nothing automatic about a child's continuance within the believing community. It is quite common for a child brought up within the community of faith to sever ties with that community as he or she grows up.

In increasingly secular Western societies, churches have had to come to terms with the notion that children's acceptance of the faith is not something which can be taken for granted. This recognition has helped concentrate minds on the quality and nature of activities for and with children within the church. Arguments over Christian initiation, for example, have often been cast in the form of what policy is best to ensure that the church 'keeps' its young people. In Anglican circles, for instance, the argument is sometimes heard that early confirmation helps retain young people as they are growing up; it is countered by the argument that later confirmation gives the opportunity for a more genuine and lasting choice on the part of the individual young person.

More positively, perhaps, the recognition of the fact that children both deserve real attention and, where they have some sort of activity of their own, need good quality materials, has led to the production of excellent published material for children, and a wealth of ideas and practical advice on working with children in a Christian context.

In chapter three we saw that when the first Christians met together, children were included. The movement in recent years from the 'Family Service' to 'All-Age Worship' has been a modern attempt to recapture something of that inclusive quality of the first Christians' worship. In many British Nonconformist churches, there has been a long-standing tradition of a children's talk towards the start of a time of worship, after which the children and adults separate for their own times of worship and teaching. These different ways of involving children – Family Service, Junior Church, All-Age Worship, or Children's Address – are all variations on the theme of including children in an appropriate way in the church's worship. In one way or another these different strategies are returning to the practice of the first Christians, and are building on it.

Recognizing the presence of children in worship is always a challenge. But a church where children are present in worship is nearer the New Testament pattern than one in which they are either not welcome at all, or in which they are relegated entirely to activities of their own. A church which not only has children present at worship, but also includes material appropriate for them, is developing the possibilities shown to us in Ephesians and Colossians (pp.73-5).

The provision of specific children's activities, such as Sunday School, weekday groups or Holiday Clubs, is of course something quite unknown to the New Testament – but only because such particular attention to the needs of children would have been hard to envisage in their culture. The first Christians could not have thought of the *means*, but they would have understood the *aim* of bringing children up to know and love the Lord. To that extent, and as far as children's separate activities remain a means of bringing children into the church, rather than a way of keeping them conveniently out of it, such activities are surely totally in accord with what the first Christians hoped for the children of the Christian community.

We have not been able to resolve the long-running disagreement about the baptism of children or infants. We saw in chapter four, though, that there is a strong case for believing that the Christian church baptized infants from the very beginning. At its best, infant baptism affirms that the child is a member of the church from the start of its life. It can help show the truth expressed in Jesus's teaching that childhood is not an apprenticeship for becoming a disciple; quite the opposite, the child shows the adult disciple what it means to be in the kingdom of God (pp.48-58). At its worst, infant baptism can become quite separated from any notion of life in the kingdom of God, or of discipleship.

Some writers on the subject have indeed tried to create a justification for an indiscriminate baptism of infants, on the grounds of grace conveyed through the rite. This is in itself a large and debatable subject, but from what we have seen of the practice and belief of the New Testament and early church, it is clear that baptism and discipleship were intimately linked. If the early church did indeed baptize infants, and the present writer's conviction is that it did, then such baptism was always a firm commitment to a life of discipleship and certainly not a social convention, a curious survival from a previous belief system, or a means of injecting grace willynilly into an infant life. After all, it was this firmly-embedded notion that baptism committed the candidate to discipleship which gave Tertullian scruples about infant baptism, and which, we have argued, began the temporary eclipse of infant baptism in the third and fourth centuries (pp.86f, 92-5). Infant baptism today, if it is to claim any realistic continuity with the baptism of the New Testament, must be closely related to a commitment to discipleship. The widespread existence of nominal church membership, a sense which many people have of 'belonging' to the church without active participation in the church's life, poses difficulties for infant-baptist churches. How do they secure that link between baptism and commitment to discipleship? Some advocates of infant baptism argue that it must be secured through the family, while others would allow that it may be established through the wider faith and nurture provided by the church, but infant baptism without that link, a rite in isolation, is not the baptism which the early Christians knew.

. Those Christians who are not persuaded that the baptism of infants is valid or right do not, of course, forget or overlook the children of the Christian community. The birth of a child is such a momentous event that some marking of the arrival is generally thought appropriate, and in many churches which practice 'believers' baptism' there is still a place for a thanksgiving or dedication ceremony for a newborn child of Christian parents. Such a ceremony could perhaps claim a precedent in the writings of Aristides in the second century (see above, pp.85f).

We have seen that the admission of children to Communion was certainly an early practice (pp.104-6), although it cannot be established beyond doubt as a practice of the New Testament itself (p.104). Churches around the world are looking afresh at the issue of children and Communion. Many are realizing that they have no reason not to open the Lord's Table to their youngest worshippers. Some still question whether children have the capacity to 'discern the body' (1 Cor.11:29), and so want to ensure that young people are only admitted to Communion at a certain stage of personal development, even if that stage is quite an early one (as with Roman Catholic practice). They would argue that some form of preparation is necessary before children are welcomed to the fellowship of the Lord's Table. Others are concerned that complete Christian initiation must include the laying-on of hands and provision of prayer for the coming of the Holy Spirit; they would therefore want to see confirmation in some form before admission to Communion. But on the whole, the admission (or, if we look far enough back into history, we should say the readmission) of children to the Communion is gaining impetus in a number of churches.

Churches have rediscovered children. A cynic might suggest that this rediscovery has been prompted by the instinct for self-preservation. An impartial observer might well point out that the churches are responding to secular thinkers such as Freud or Piaget. But the Christian church can legitimately give attention to children precisely because they feature so clearly in its own foundational texts. Christians inherited from Judaism a positive attitude to their children. Jesus' interest in children and concern for them could never be totally overlooked by his disciples. And the early church left behind eloquent testimony to the care it took to bring children up 'in the Lord'. The churches could rediscover children because the resources for that rediscovery were always there.

Children and the family

The traditional teaching of the early church was that the child would be nurtured within the family, spiritually as well as physically (pp.73-83).

The churches used the household as their basic building blocks. Today, at least in many Western societies, the family itself is in need of nurture, and the church can make fewer assumptions about the composition and nature of the household. Because work is seldom done from home, and the household has become a unit of consumption only (in contrast to the ancient family, which was often a unit both of production *and* consumption), the time a modern family spends together is often limited, with all the stresses that result from this limitation. Poverty places further stresses on family life, as does the responsibility for the growing numbers of elderly family members In addition, the definition of a family is no longer as clear as it once was. In all these ways, and more, the 'family' is becoming a focus of growing concern (see, for a brief but penetrating analysis of the transformation of the family in modern culture, Vasey 1995 27–37).

It is no new observation that the family needs support. One of the guiding principles of the Mothers' Union within the Anglican church for over a century has been to foster family life through helping mothers in particular. In more recent years a large number of organizations, programmes and publications have appeared, from all Christian traditions, with the aim of supporting the family. Christian care for children has issued in many practical enterprises to help families to cope, springing from the recognition that the well-being of children is dependent on the functioning of the households to which they belong. Christians cannot, therefore, be indifferent to the state of the family, especially when children's welfare is in question.

The New Testament material which we examined in chapter three (pp.73-7) gives us the outlines of a *policy* for the Christian family and a *possibility* for the Christian family.

The *policy* is seen in the Pastoral Epistles. It was marked by a strong call to conform to social norms and ethical expectations. Its aim was to produce well-regulated household units, which contemporaries could recognize and admire. In this respect, the family unit, and children within it, had an apologetic value in commending the faith (Tit.2:4f.) as well as an intrinsic importance in the care of the young. In a less hierarchical age, we should be careful not to dismiss this approach too lightly. It was, after all, the dominant strand of thinking on family life in early Christianity. As those who live in an age of radical instability within the family unit, it is important for us to be reminded that stability and order within the household are valuable and important, for adults as much as for children.

This policy for the family had its eye on two further goals: well-ordered households would commend the Christian message, and would help ensure the nurture of the coming generation of believers.

The *possibility*, on the other hand, was a vision of Christian growth as an end in itself. It is seen most clearly in Ephesians 5:21–6:9, with the household as a community of Christ-like love, in which members are bound to one another by a mutual self-giving. The roles of obedience and discipline are still recognizable, but the language of control and order is replaced by that of service and mutual care. The possibility contained in this material is that of making the family itself a practical working example of the living body of Christ. Ephesians says that all fatherhood (or family) derives from the Father, and expands on this statement to show how this fatherhood leads to enrichment, strengthening and growth (Eph.4:14–21). Human fatherhood (or family) is to lead to the same open-ended possibilities.

How do we evaluate this New Testament and post-New Testament material on the family today? Some Christian writers have taken this hierarchical model as normative. They would argue that the husband and father has a God-given authority within the home, with the wife and mother in a subordinate position, and the children below the two adults. But concentrating on the language of control and management which we find in some strands of the New Testament may lead us away from the New Testament's key insights. It may make us give too much attention to a culture-bound *policy*, while we neglect the more profound *possibilities* for the family and for children found elsewhere, and particularly in Ephesians.

The testimony of Ephesians brings us back to the teaching of Jesus himself, in which we saw a clear relativizing of the place of the family (pp.59-61). The claims of family are not absolute. They are to take second place to the claims of the kingdom of God. Ephesians makes the same point in a different way: its teaching on the family does not merely reinforce the common view of the hierarchical family, but views all members of the household as disciples together. Instead of accepting the structure of the household as a given, and building the church out of these existing blocks, Ephesians (and Colossians more briefly: Col.3:18–4:1) introduces the leaven of the kingdom of God within the interior life of the family, for the family, too, is to be transformed 'in Christ'.

Parents still have to be parents, and children are still children. But the way in which those roles are performed could be radically changed by the mutual care which is enjoined on the church by Ephesians and

Colossians. From these letters we also see that children have their own discipleship, something we recognize from the teaching of Jesus on children. The early Christians subsumed children's discipleship under that of their parents (pp.74-9), largely because of their confidence in the household as a building block of the church. It may well be that, ironically, contemporary Christians' *lack* of confidence in the family is leading to an over-emphasis on the family unit, but with the same eventual effect that the child's status as a disciple disappears behind the family.

Just as the churches' interest in children has been prompted in part by the realization that their young people are leaving the community of faith, so too the churches' interest in the family has been in part stimulated by a sense of crisis, a feeling that the family as an institution is not functioning well in practice, and is subject to increasing criticism in theory. To attempt to resolve this crisis about the family simply by reaffirming a hierarchical model of family life may be to mistake the *necessary form* which the church evolved in order to survive for the *essential substance* of the New Testament's key insights. Those insights, in fact, point away from a purely authoritarian structure for the family, and towards a partnership of mutual obligation and growth in Christ with one another.

Our concern here has been with children in particular, rather than with the family as an institution – a huge topic in itself. But children's experience of family life is enormously varied. Many children in Western communities will be living in lone-parent households, or find their lives divided between one parent (typically a mother) with whom they spend most of their time, and a second parent (typically a father) whom they see occasionally. Relationships with step-parents are a common and complicating element in their lives. What does our New Testament material have to say about this? We might suggest that what we have called the 'policy' reminds and urges us that stability within the household, however difficult to create and maintain, remains important, and should not be surrendered as a goal and ideal. We might recognize, further, that the 'possibility' both reassures and challenges us with the recognition that the quality and Christlikeness of our family relationships are more profoundly important than the particular patterns which these relationships assume.

Children remain children in the kingdom of God, and Jesus' approach to children through their parents was one noticeable feature of the gospel record (pp.62-5). Parents still have the responsibility to 'bring children up in the discipline and instruction of the Lord' (Eph 6:4). And the church today needs to reaffirm the constant theme of the early church that parents take seriously their vital role in leading their children in prayer and discipleship.

Final Conclusion

Our brief consideration of children, the church and the family today, has reminded us that when we as adults think about children and how we care for them we are brought to think about ourselves and our discipleship. If the leaven of the kingdom of God is to work anywhere, it has to work everywhere, including our homes and families.

By drawing attention to children, speaking of them, healing them, commending them as examples and objects of care, Jesus handed to his followers a responsibility to give children a central place in their life together. In changing circumstances, the way in which that responsibility is discharged will change. We may not today do things exactly as the early church did them. But the challenge to make children a priority has lost none of its urgency with the passage of time. A church which is faithful to its Lord will show its faithfulness in no clearer way than by its love for children, for whom he cared so deeply.

Bibliography

Aland, K. *Did the Early Church Baptize Infants?*, SCM (London), 1963

Barr, J. ' "Abba" isn't "Daddy" ' *Journal of Theological Studies,* 39 (1988), 28–47

Barton, S.C. *Discipleship and Family Ties in Mark and Matthew*, Society for New Testament. Monograph Series 80. Cambridge University Press (Cambridge), 1994

Beasley-Murray, G.R. *Baptism in the New Testament,* Paternoster Press (Carlisle), 1972

Binfield. C. 'The Purley way for Children', in D. Wood (ed), *The Church and Childhood* (Studies in Church History 31), Basil Blackwell (Oxford), 1994, 461–76

Bingham, R. (ed), *The Works of the Rev. Joseph Bingham, 10 vols,* Oxford University Press (Oxford), 1855

Bowen, J. *A History of Western Education,* 1: *The Ancient World*, Methuen (London), 1972

Bowman, A.K. and Thomas, J.D. *The Vindolanda Writing-Tablets* (Tabulae Vindolandenses II), British Museum press (London), 1994

Brown, R.E. *The Birth of the Messiah*, Geoffrey Chapman (London), 2nd edn 1993

Carcopino, J. *Daily Life in Ancient Rome*, Penguin (Harmondsworth), 1956

Cliff, P.B. *The Rise and Development of the Sunday School Movement in England 1780–1980*, (Redhill), 1986

Diehl, E. (ed.), *Inscriptiones latinae christianae veteres*, 3 vols (Berlin), 1925–31

Ellis, I. 'Jesus and the Subversive Family', *Scottish Journal of Theology* 38 (1985), 173–88

Fox, R.L. *Christians and Pagans*, Penguin (Harmondsworth), 1986

Green, M. *Baptism*, Hodder and Stoughton (London), 1987

Hefele, J. and Leclerq, H. *Histoire des Conciles*, (11 vols in 22 parts) Letouzey & Ané (Paris) 1907–52

Holeton, D. *Infant Communion Then and Now*, Grove Books (Nottingham), 1981

Jeremias, J. *Infant Baptism in the First Four Centuries*, SCM (London), 1960

Jeremias, J. *The Origins of Infant Baptism*, SCM (London), 1963

Kleijwegt, M. *Ancient Youth: The ambiguity of youth and the absence of adolescence in Greco-Roman Society* (Dutch Monographs on Ancient History and Archaeology 8), J.C. Gieben (Amsterdam), 1991

Laqueur, T.W. *Religion and Respectability: Sunday Schools and Working Class Culture 1780–1850*, (Yale), 1976

Laistner, M.L.W. *Christianity and Pagan Culture in the Later Roman Empire*, Cornell University Press (Ithaca, NY), 1951

Marrou, H-I, *A History of Education in Antiquity*, Sheed and Ward (London/New York), 1956

DeMause, L. (ed), *The History of Childhood*, Souvenir Press (London), 1974

Musurillo, H. *The Acts of the Christian Martyrs*, Clarendon Press (Oxford), 1972

Rawson, B. 'The Roman Family', in B.Rawson (ed), *The Family in Ancient Rome. New Perspectives*, Croom Helm (London/Sydney), 1986, 1–57

Rawson, B. 'Adult-Child Relationships in Roman Society', in B. Rawson (ed), *Marriage Divorce and Children in Ancient Rome*, Humanities Research Centre/Clarendon Press (Canberra/Oxford) 1991, 7–30

Riddle, J.M. 'Oral Contraceptives and Early-Term Abortifacients during Classical Antiquity and the Middle Ages', *Past and Present* 132 (1991), 3–32

Rousselle, A. *Porneia. On Desire and the Body in Antiquity*, Basil Blackwell (Oxford), 1988

Safrai, S. and Stern, M. (eds), *The Jewish People in the First Century* (Compendia Rerum Iudiacarum ad Novum Testamentum 1), Van Gorcum (Assen/Amsterdam), 1976

Stevenson, J. *A New Eusebius. Documents illustrating the history of the Church to AD 337*, New Edn. revised by W.H.C. Frend, SPCK (London), 1987

Strack, H.L. and Billerbeck, P. *Kommentar zum Neuen Testament aus Talmud und Midrasch*, 6 vols in 7, C.H. Beck (Munich), 1922–61

Treggiari, S. *Roman Marriage. Iusti Coniuges from the Time of Cicero to the Time of Ulpian*, Clarendon Press (Oxford), 1991

Vasey, M. *Strangers and Friends, a new exploration of homosexuality and the Bible*, Hodder and Stoughton (London), 1995

Verner, D.C. *The Household of God. The Social World of the Pastoral Epistles* (Society of Biblical Literature, Dissertation Series 71), Scholars Press (Chico, California), 1983

Wiedemann, T. *Adults and Children in the Roman Empire*, Routledge (London), 1989

Wise, M.O. 'Languages of Palestine', in J.B. Green and S. McKnight (eds), *Dictionary of Jesus and the Gospels*, Inter-Varsity Press (Leicester/Downers Grove, Ill.), 1992, 434–444

Witherington, B. III, 'Birth of Jesus', in J.B. Green and S.McKnight (eds), *Dictionary of Jesus and the Gospels*, Inter-Varsity Press (Leicester/Downers Grove, Ill.), 1992, 60–74

Yates, A.S. *Why Baptize Infants? A study of the biblical, traditional and theological evidence*, Canterbury Press (Norwich), 1993